GOOD FRIENDS, GREAT DINNERS

GOOD FRIENDS, GREAT DINNERS

32 Menus for Casual Entertaining

SUSAN COSTNER

With Camilla Turnbull

Photographs by Faith Echtermeyer

CROWN PUBLISHERS, INC. · NEW YORK

Grateful acknowledgment is made for permission to use the following recipes:

"Lamb Moghul" (page 22) by Gary Danko.

"Giant Popovers" (page 32) and "Stuffed Dates with Caramel Sauce" (page 142) by Julie Wagner.

"Spa Chocolate Mousse". (page 40) by Terry Richards, Sonoma Mission Inn, Sonoma, California.

"San Francisco Earthquake Cake" or "Torta Terramoto" (page 61) by Carlo Middione and Mirella Nasi, Vivande Porta Via Restaurant, San Francisco, California.

"Mushrooms Cooked in Grape Leaves" (page 77) from *Summer Cooking* by Elizabeth David. Copyright © 1980 by Elizabeth David. Used by permission of Jill Norman Limited and Elizabeth David.

"Crepinettes" (page 104) by Bruce Aidells, Aidell's Sausage Company, Kensington, California.

"*Fougasse* with Rosemary" (page 128) by Karen Mitchell, the Model Bakery, St. Helena, California.

"Sizzling Carrots" (page 196) by Devon Fredericks.

"Chocolate-Cranberry Torte" (page 206) from *The Ark Restaurant Cookbook* by Jimella Lucas and Nanci Main. Copyright © 1983 by Ladysmith Limited Publishing Company. Used by permission of Ladysmith Limited Publishing Company, St. Louis, Missouri.

Grateful acknowledgment is made to Thomas Bartlett for permission to reproduce photographs of the interior and exterior of his lovely home.

Published by Crown Publishers, Inc.
225 Park Avenue South, New York, New York 10003
and represented in Canada by the Canadian MANDA Group
CROWN is a trademark of Crown Publishers, Inc.

Manufactured in Japan
Design by Nancy Kenmore

Library of Congress Cataloging-in-Publication Data
Costner, Susan.
Good friends, great dinners.
Includes index.
1. Dinners and dining.   2. Menus.   I. Title.
TX737.C65   1987   642'.4   86-16829
ISBN 0-517-56505-6

10   9   8   7   6   5   4   3   2   1
First Edition

To Tor
Who Cooked Up the Best Thing
With Love

Contents

FALL

WINTER

Acknowledgments

*F*irst and foremost, love and thanks to my dear friend Camilla Turnbull, for her unpressured advice, constant encouragement, and reassuring presence . . . again, *sine qua non.*

And thanks again to my friend and editor Pamela Thomas for doing what she does best.

To Faith Echtermeyer, who did all the beautiful photography throughout the book—and for so much more, especially acclimating me to California.

To Joan Comendant for being unfailingly available and patient, and a jack of all trades.

To John Nyquist, Charles Gautreaux, and Kathy Vanderbilt at Vanderbilt and Company in St. Helena, California, who generously supplied all the beautiful linens, dishes, and accessories you see page after page.

To Susan Smith for getting me to and keeping me in St. Helena; for sharing her house, her things, her family, and her friends.

To Gary Danko for his recipes and expert knowledge.

To Phil Rogers for his advice on beer selections.

To everyone at the Oakville Grocery for answering my constant questions, and to Ernie Navone at Keller's Market, and Dick Warton at St. Helena Fish Market for the same reason.

To all my new friends in St. Helena who so graciously welcomed me into their homes and gardens and allowed me to invade their cabinets and use their possessions when we were photographing. Especially my neighbors Jean McNabb Rothlin and Julie and Gary Wagner, who saw, smelled, and tasted it all, and to the Sparks, the Dakes, the Cunninghams, Lila Jeager, Thomas Bartlett, Ann Cutting, Boris Lakusta, Bernice Bradley, and the Eldridges, and to Belle Rhodes for use of her library.

And finally, to Seana McGowan and Paula Presley for keeping pace with their rapid and accurate typing.

An Invitation to Friends

*I*n her book *Gastronomical Me,* M.F.K. Fisher formulated her equation for happy dining. "I feel now," she wrote, "that gastronomical perfection can be reached in these combinations: one person dining alone, usually upon a couch or a hillside; two people of no matter what sex or age, dining in a good restaurant; six people, of no matter what sex or age, dining in a good home." This is a book in answer to the last combination, a book for people who enjoy cooking in their homes for their friends. For me, there is nothing more relaxing than sharing a meal with close friends, especially in my own home, where I can keep things easygoing and comfortable.

All of the menus in this book are for M.F.K. Fisher's magic number of six. Six is ideal. Cooking for six people is no more complicated than cooking for four; as soon as you move up to eight, you have a full-fledged "Dinner Party" on your hands, an event that catapults many a host or hostess into general panic and killing self-consciousness. Besides, six people fit neatly around a table and conversation remains intimate.

It has been said that restaurants are the new theater. Perhaps so. But do you want to be a supporting actor in a theatrical production when you are eating with your friends? Restaurants are fine if you want to "be seen," entertain at a business lunch, or furnish a celebration dinner; but people talk and behave differently in a public restaurant than they do in a private home. They are less relaxed and less revealing about themselves. The food is less personal. Real friendships are best nurtured over a home-cooked meal.

I started cooking in Sagaponack, Long Island, back in the mid-1970s as co-owner, with my longtime friend Devon Fredericks, of a small shoebox of a store situated right in the middle of the celebrated Hamptons. The store was called Loaves and Fishes, a biblical expression meaning "godsend." Our customers, who came from all over the world to our doorstep, had discerning and voracious appetites, and it was a constant challenge to satisfy them. Before there was a Dean & DeLuca or a Silver Palate, Loaves and Fishes was out there in the potato fields, one of the very first of the gourmet take-out food shops that have sprung up in most cities and major towns throughout the country. Now I live in California's Napa Valley, in one of the great wine-producing regions of the world, with an embarrassingly vast variety of fresh fruits and vegetables available almost year-round. It is a veritable cook's paradise.

Now that I've been in the food business for ten years, I would like to share with you, by way of *Good Friends, Great Dinners,* some of the secrets I have learned through my experiences. I believe in doing as little work as possible; therefore, I have simplified elaborate step-by-step preparations and eliminated tedious or needless work while retaining the essence and integrity of a dish. Cooking for friends at home should be relaxed, simple, enjoyable, and comfortable. Excessive attention to food and its preparation can, when extreme, border on the absurd and the distinctly *un*comfortable. Arabella Boxer, one of England's great cooks and food writers, diagnosed this tendency in the introduction to *Arabella Boxer's Book of Elegant Cooking and Entertaining:* "Exaggerated activities fill me with apprehension, for they seem to have more to do with exhibitionism than hospitality. The desire to give pleasure to one's friends can soon deteriorate into a demand for applause." Finicky "presentation" can also be tiresome. Dishes that have been "painted" on a plate belong in three-star restaurants. An attractive, welcoming table, however, is another matter; a pretty tablecloth, oversize napkins, flowers, and candles are real necessities and always heighten the enjoyment of a meal.

The menus here have been designed for the discerning cook who has a life outside the kitchen and whose kitchen, furthermore, is not arrayed like a restaurant kitchen in miniature. Most of these recipes demand no extraordinary skill or unusual equipment: One does not need a restaurant stove, an elaborate *batterie de cuisine,* or (most unlikely of all) a staff, though a few friends pitching in at the last minute can be a significant bonus. Some technical know-how is helpful, but I have tried to keep things within the reach of the less-experienced cook. I stress the importance of using the freshest and best ingredients possible, and, if necessary, changing a pre-set menu to accommodate them. The emphasis is on lighter fare—fish, chicken, grilled meats, and lots of vegetables.

The 32 menus are divided according to seasons and each is organized around a main dish. When approaching a menu in a given season, you might say, "Something with fish would be nice" or "What's a good way to have chicken now?" So it is useful to refer to a seasonal menu featuring poultry or fish or beef, depending on your choice. In keeping with the temper of the times, I have included a vegetarian menu for each season. The menus are intended merely as guidelines, taking into account what is freshest and best. Feel free to juggle them around at your whim. This is what will make the book personal for you. After all, your spot on the globe may not have fresh chanterelles in the fall but *may* have some other local specialty I have never dreamed of.

Finally, I have taken full advantage of the revived American cuisine that has captured our national imagination. My own style of cooking is greatly influenced by my Southern upbringing in Virginia and North Carolina. It also reflects the pleasurable eating experiences I have had in my travels across America, as well as on my trips to Europe. Over the years I have picked up recipes, methods, ideas, and enthusiasms from anywhere and everywhere, for that really is my way of doing things.

—Susan Costner

St. Helena, California

"I don't especially enjoy going out to evenings where someone gets up and performs—or where there's entertainment. I much prefer talk. Good conversation is rare and becoming increasingly so. It's totally wonderful when you can experience an evening at someone's house—a small, intimate gathering—where a good talker takes over and stimulates a good argument. Good cooks, jolly fellows— that's what make a dinner."
DIANA VREELAND

Spring Chickens

M·e·n·u

WARM
CHICKEN LIVER SALAD
WITH SUGAR SNAP PEAS

·

ROASTED POUSSIN
WITH MUSHROOM-WALNUT SAUCE

·

QUICK-COOK SPINACH

·

SAUTÉED RADISHES

·

A CHOCOLATE CAKE
FOR DENNIS

We wait for spring so long through the endless days of winter and then, when it finally arrives, time seems to accelerate and we are hurtled along, too fast, toward summer. There is scarcely time to sample all the sweet and subtle delicacies that come with this favorite and fleeting season. My Spring Chicken menu attempts to ensure you the taste of at least a few of them. If the evening is warm enough, sit on an open porch and savor the soft, fragile scents on the air and the return of color in the first flowers.

This is basically a roast chicken dinner dressed up in fashionable clothes. The diminutive poussin, so very delicious, is a distinct variety of chicken, fully mature and ready to eat at three weeks, weighing about a pound.

ORDER OF PREPARATION

Some last-minute cooking is the only tricky part of this meal. Begin by preparing the cake the day before or early in the morning. You may cook the rice and get it out of the way while the cake is baking.

An hour and a half before the guests arrive, wash and trim the spinach, radishes, and peas. Make the sauce for the chicken up to the point where you add the egg yolks and cream. Chop and toss the stuffing, fill the poussins. Three quarters of an hour before dinner, put the birds in the oven.

The crunch occurs just before you sit down. Marshal your forces. The warm chicken liver salad should be made just before you are ready to eat it. After you serve the salad, sauté the spinach and radishes and finish the sauce for the poussins. Each guest should be served one whole poussin with a little sauce and some vegetables.

Dust the chocolate cake with confectioners' sugar just before serving.

Wine suggestion: Serve a rich, flavorful Chardonnay.

WARM CHICKEN LIVER SALAD WITH SUGAR SNAP PEAS

SERVES 6

¾ pound sugar snap peas,
tipped and tailed
Salt
6 tablespoons hazelnut or
walnut oil
4 tablespoons white wine
vinegar

4 slices bacon
¾ pound chicken livers, cut
in half with stringy parts
removed
Freshly ground black
pepper to taste

Blanch the peas in 2 quarts of salted boiling water until just tender, 2 to 3 minutes. Drain. Whisk together the nut oil and vinegar and pour over the peas. Keep warm in a heated bowl.

In a medium-size skillet, cook the bacon until crisp; then drain, crumble, and set aside. Season the chicken livers with salt and pepper and sauté in the hot bacon fat until crisp but still pink on the inside, 3 to 4 minutes. Toss the warm livers and crumbled bacon with the peas and serve immediately.

SUGAR SNAP PEAS. It was a great day when plant hybridizers came up with the sugar snap. A real breakthrough, this variety has delicately sweet peas you can serve raw or steamed, or you can cook and eat them, pod and all, as you would a snow pea. Fresh peas herald the spring and there are few garden rewards as delicious.

ROASTED POUSSIN WITH MUSHROOM-WALNUT SAUCE

SERVES 6

STUFFING
2 cups cooked white or
brown rice
½ cup coarsely chopped dried
apricots
½ cup finely chopped celery
⅓ cup finely chopped
scallions
½ cup coarsely chopped
mushrooms
¼ cup coarsely chopped
walnuts

¼ cup finely chopped fresh
parsley
Salt and freshly ground
black pepper to taste

6 12- to 16-ounce poussins
3 tablespoons unsalted
butter, melted
A dusting of paprika

Mushroom-Walnut Sauce
(recipe follows)

*Y*ou can substitute squab, quail, or Cornish hen in this recipe, although I think the poussin is most succulent and flavorful.

Preheat the oven to 325° F.

To make the stuffing, combine all the ingredients in a bowl and toss well.

Bring the poussins to room temperature. Divide the stuffing evenly between the birds, packing it loosely in the cavities. Tie the legs together. Brush the skin all over with the melted butter. Sprinkle a little paprika over the skin and rub it in well, more to improve the finished color than for flavor. Put the birds in a roasting pan and roast for 40 to 45 minutes or until the legs move easily and the juices run clear.

Serve 1 whole poussin per person with some of the Mushroom-Walnut Sauce poured over it.

"*P*oultry
is for the cook what canvas is for the
painter."
BRILLAT-SAVARIN

MUSHROOM-WALNUT SAUCE

SERVES 6

3 tablespoons unsalted
   butter
¼ cup minced shallots
6 ounces white mushrooms,
   finely chopped
½ cup dried porcini
   mushrooms or
   chanterelles, soaked in 1
   cup warm water for 20
   minutes

¾ cup coarsely chopped
   walnuts, some left whole
3 tablespoons freshly
   squeezed lemon juice
3 large egg yolks, beaten
1 cup heavy cream
   Salt and freshly ground
   black pepper to taste

Melt the butter in a medium-size saucepan. Add the shallots and cook until translucent. Add the white mushrooms, porcini mushrooms, drained of their liquid, and walnuts. Sauté over medium-high heat until the liquid released from the mushrooms has evaporated.

Combine the lemon juice, egg yolks, and cream and stir into the mushroom mixture. Cook over low heat until thickened; do not let it boil or it will separate. Season with salt and pepper. If the sauce becomes too thick, thin it with a little of the pan drippings from the poussins or a little carefully strained mushroom soaking liquid.

QUICK-COOK SPINACH

SERVES 6

2 pounds fresh spinach with
   stems removed, washed well
2 whole garlic cloves,
   smashed and peeled

2 tablespoons olive oil or
   unsalted butter
   Salt and freshly ground
   black pepper to taste

Cook the spinach in a covered saucepan over medium heat with only the water that clings to the leaves after washing. Toss frequently. Place the garlic cloves on the prongs of a fork and swirl them through the spinach. Discard the garlic and season the spinach with the olive oil and salt and pepper. Serve hot.

SAUTÉED RADISHES

SERVES 6

2 bunches fresh red radishes
   with leaves removed,
   washed well
3 tablespoons unsalted butter

1 teaspoon coarse salt
   Freshly ground black
   pepper to taste

In a skillet, sauté the radishes in the butter over medium heat until tender, 3 to 4 minutes. Season with salt and pepper and stir again. Serve hot.

"Both eggs and seeds for planting can be tested by the same method: A good seed or a good egg sinks to the bottom of a pan of water. Those that float should be discarded."
KAY AND MARSHALL LEE
The Illuminated Book of Days

OPPOSITE: Roasted poussin with rice stuffing —these roasted miniature fowl are truly a bird-in-the-hand size.

One of the best ways to please friends is to remember what they like to eat, invite them to dinner, and serve it. Dennis Fife, a friend from St. Helena, likes chocolate cake, "the kind you need a forklift to eat." This one is slightly more delicate than his image suggests, but it is nonetheless well suited for a confirmed chocoholic.

A CHOCOLATE CAKE FOR DENNIS

SERVES 6 TO 8

6 ounces semisweet
  chocolate, broken into
  small pieces
½ cup (1 stick) unsalted
  butter
¾ cup granulated sugar
½ teaspoon salt

4 large eggs, separated
½ cup finely chopped pecans
½ teaspoon baking powder
  Confectioners' sugar for
  dusting
  Whipped cream or vanilla
  ice cream (optional)

Preheat the oven to 350° F.

Butter the bottom and sides of a 9-inch springform pan. Line the bottom with wax paper; then butter the wax paper. Flour the pan, shaking out any excess.

Melt the chocolate in a small covered saucepan over low heat. Remove from the heat and beat in the butter a little at a time until thoroughly blended. Transfer to a mixing bowl, stir in the sugar and salt, and mix until smooth. Add the egg yolks, one at a time, beating well after each addition. Combine the chopped nuts and baking powder and carefully fold them into the chocolate mixture.

Beat the egg whites in a large bowl until stiff but not dry. Stir one quarter of the chocolate mixture into the egg whites. Then, gently and lightly, fold the egg whites into the remaining chocolate mixture.

Pour into the prepared pan and bake for 30 minutes. Lower the oven temperature to 250° F. and bake for 15 to 20 minutes more. The cake will be slightly soft in the center.

Cool the cake in the pan for 10 minutes. Remove the rim and invert the cake onto a serving plate lined with a paper doily. Remove the wax paper and dust the cake with confectioners' sugar. Decorate with fresh spring violets.

If you are someone who must have icing on your cakes, use the chocolate buttercream on page 208. Serve the cake with a dollop of whipped cream or vanilla ice cream.

Spring into Lamb

Spring's lengthening days draw us once again to predinner gatherings around the backyard grill. I don't think it's an exaggeration to say that these informal get-togethers are often the most memorable of the year. This menu, featuring spirited light fare, is one of my favorites. The tender, young butterflied lamb—and spring lamb is the obvious choice for the year's first barbecue—is delectable and easy to prepare; it should come off the grill crisp and blackened on the outside, still pink and juicy on the inside. Serve plenty of good peasanty bread to soak up the juice. All the ingredients for this dish are familiar but treated in an East Indian way. Let tall glasses of ruby-hued hibiscus cooler laced with wine or spirits inspire a toast to good friends and the weatherman's generosity.

M·e·n·u

SPRING TONIC

·

LAMB MOGHUL

·

SAUTÉED
CHERRY TOMATOES

·

SPINACH
WITH CHICK-PEAS

·

LAVOSH FLAT BREAD
OR PITA

·

HIBISCUS COOLER

·

FRESH COCONUT CAKE
WITH RASPBERRY PURÉE

ORDER OF PREPARATION

Marinate the lamb for at least 2 days. Turn it several times a day while it marinates. Make the cake as well as the raspberry purée in advance. Well before dinner, make and chill the soup and the hibiscus cooler.

An hour before friends are due, start the grill and wash and prepare the vegetables. There are many variables in cooking on the grill, so be prepared to add more coals if your guests are late or choose to linger over the "tonic."

Don't forget to add the club soda to the soup before serving it. Put the lamb on the grill a few minutes before you serve the soup. When you turn the lamb, finish the vegetables. Let the lamb rest for 10 minutes before slicing it. For dessert, serve the cake with coffee and more hibiscus cooler.

Wine suggestion: In place of, or in addition to, the hibiscus cooler, offer a medium-bodied Merlot.

SPRING TONIC

SERVES 6

2 cucumbers, peeled
1 small carrot, peeled and
    finely grated
2 scallions, white part only,
    finely chopped
1/4 cup chopped fresh mint
1 garlic clove, peeled
1 quart plain yogurt or
    buttermilk

1 pint sour cream
1 teaspoon salt
2 tablespoons freshly
    squeezed lemon juice
3/4 cup club soda
GARNISH
    Freshly ground black
    pepper
    Chopped fresh parsley

Cut 6 paper-thin slices from 1 cucumber and set them aside. Cut the cucumbers in half lengthwise; scoop out the seeds and discard them. Cut the cucumbers into small pieces.

In a blender or food processor, place half of the chopped cucumber, half the grated carrot, half the scallions, half the mint, and all the garlic. Moisten with 2 cups of the yogurt and blend until smooth. Pour the puréed mixture into a large serving pitcher or bowl and whisk in the remaining yogurt, sour cream, salt, and lemon juice. Fold in the remaining vegetables and mint. Cover and chill thoroughly.

Just before serving, stir in the club soda. Garnish each bowl or mug with a reserved cucumber slice, a grinding of pepper, and some chopped parsley.

This inspired variation on grilled butterflied leg of lamb is a wonderful recipe created by Gary Danko, one of America's great up-and-coming chefs. It is best grilled outdoors though you could do it under the broiler. Leftovers taste superb the next day.

LAMB MOGHUL

SERVES 6

1 7- to 8-pound leg of
    spring lamb, butterflied
MARINADE
    3 cups plain yogurt
    Juice of 6 limes
    2 teaspoons minced fresh
        ginger
    4 1/2 teaspoons coarse salt
    1 1/2 teaspoons cayenne pepper

3 tablespoons coriander
    seeds
1 1/2 teaspoons ground
    cinnamon
1 1/2 teaspoons ground cloves
1 1/2 teaspoons ground
    cardamom
1 teaspoon freshly ground
    black pepper

Carefully cut away all the fat and tissue from the meat; make several slits on both sides with a sharp knife. Put the lamb in a noncorrodible roasting pan.

Combine the marinade ingredients in a bowl and pour over the lamb. Cover and refrigerate for at least 2 days, turning the meat at least three or four times during this period.

Remove the lamb from the refrigerator and bring to room temperature. Prepare a large charcoal fire, and when the coals are medium-hot, remove the lamb from the marinade and grill it about 4 inches above the coals for 5 to 8 minutes on each side to sear and seal; then raise the grill several inches and grill for about 10 to 15 minutes

more on each side—about 30 to 40 minutes total grilling time. Brush the lamb frequently with the marinade. The lamb is best black on the outside and pink on the inside. Let the meat rest for 10 minutes to collect the juices before slicing it. Slice on the diagonal and spoon some of the marinade over the meat.

ABOVE: Lamb Moghul with sautéed cherry tomatoes, spinach with chick-peas, and lavosh flatbread

SAUTÉED CHERRY TOMATOES

SERVES 6

1 pint cherry tomatoes with stems removed, washed
3 tablespoons olive oil
1 garlic clove, peeled and minced

½ teaspoon coarse salt or to taste
2 tablespoons finely chopped fresh parsley

With a small sharp knife, cut a small cross in the stem end of each tomato. Put the tomatoes in a single layer in a medium-size saucepan. Add the oil and garlic and sprinkle with the salt. Sauté over low heat until the tomatoes are just heated through, about 5 minutes, stirring gently several times. Sprinkle with the parsley and serve hot.

LAVOSH FLATBREAD is a gigantic and most dramatic-looking 18-inch round Armenian cracker—perfect for soaking up the lamb marinade. It can be purchased at Armenian grocery stores or gourmet food shops.

SPINACH WITH CHICK-PEAS

SERVES 6

1 garlic clove, peeled and
  minced
½ small onion, finely
  chopped
2 tablespoons olive oil
4 pounds fresh spinach with
  stems removed, washed
1 cup bottled chili sauce
  Pinch of cayenne pepper

1 10-ounce can chick-peas,
  drained of the liquid
  (Reserve ¼ cup of the
  liquid and rinse peas well
  under cold water.)
⅛ teaspoon saffron threads,
  crumbled
  Salt and freshly ground
  black pepper to taste

In a large saucepan, sauté the garlic and onion in the oil until golden. Add the spinach, cover, and cook, tossing frequently, until the spinach is just wilted. Add the chili sauce, cayenne pepper, drained chick-peas and reserved liquid, and saffron. Cover and simmer until bubbly. Season with salt and pepper.

HIBISCUS COOLER

SERVES 6

6 tablespoons or 6 tea bags
  hibiscus or Red Zinger tea
  Crushed ice
  Sugar to taste
  White wine, such as Vouvray,
  or vodka or gin to taste

3 cups club soda or sparkling
  mineral water
GARNISH
  Lemon or lime slices

Steep the tea in 3 cups of hot water for at least 5 minutes. Cool completely. Half-fill a large pitcher with crushed ice, pour in the hibiscus tea; then add the sugar and wine or liquor to taste. Stir the mixture and then add the club soda. Garnish with lemon or lime slices.

FRESH COCONUT CAKE
WITH RASPBERRY PURÉE

SERVES 6 TO 8

3 cups cake flour, sifted
1 tablespoon baking
  powder
½ teaspoon salt
½ cup (1 stick) unsalted
  butter
¼ cup liquid shortening
1 cup sugar
4 large eggs, separated
1 teaspoon vanilla extract

¾ cup fresh coconut milk
2½ cups freshly grated
  coconut

½ cup Lemon Curd (recipe
  follows)

Seven-Minute Frosting
  (recipe follows)

Raspberry Purée (page 26)

"Non-cooks
think it's silly to invest two hours' work in
two minutes' enjoyment; but if cooking is
evanescent, well, so is the ballet."
JULIA CHILD

Preheat the oven to 350° F. Generously butter two 9-inch-round cake pans and line the bottoms with wax paper; then butter the wax paper.

In a bowl, sift together the flour, baking powder, and salt; set aside.

In another bowl, cream the butter and shortening together; then add the sugar and continue beating until light and fluffy. Add the egg yolks one at a time, beating well after each addition; then add the vanilla. Add the dry ingredients alternating with the coconut milk, beating until smooth after each addition. Fold in 1 cup of the coconut.

In a medium-size bowl, beat the egg whites until stiff but not dry. Gently fold the egg whites into the batter with a rubber spatula. Divide the batter evenly between the two prepared pans and bake for 35 to 40 minutes or until the cake pulls away from sides of the pans. Cool on wire racks for 10 minutes; then remove the cakes from the pans and place them on the wire racks to cool completely. Remove wax paper.

Toast the remaining 1½ cups of coconut in the oven until lightly brown, stirring frequently.

To assemble the cake, brush all crumbs from the cake layers. Put 1 layer on a serving plate and spread it with the lemon curd. Stack the remaining layer on top. Frost the entire cake with Seven-Minute Frosting and cover the top and sides of the cake with the toasted coconut. Serve with the Raspberry Purée.

LEMON CURD

MAKES 3 CUPS

5 large eggs
2 cups sugar

10 tablespoons (1¼ sticks)
unsalted butter, melted
4 lemons

In a large bowl, beat the eggs at high speed witih an electric mixer until thick and lemon-colored. Gradually add the sugar, beating well after each addition. Add the melted butter in a steady stream, beating all the time.

Finely grate the rind from 3 of the lemons. Add their juice and the grated rind to the mixture and beat well.

Transfer the mixture to the top of a double boiler set over hot water on medium heat. Cook, uncovered, stirring constantly, for approximately 10 minutes. Cool. Store the curd in sterilized canning jars in the refrigerator for up to one week. Use it to make lemon tarts or as a spread for scones, muffins, biscuits, or even waffles.

SEVEN-MINUTE FROSTING

MAKES 4 CUPS

1½ cups sugar
2 large egg whites

¼ teaspoon cream of tartar
¼ cup ice water

Combine the ingredients in the top of a double boiler set over boiling water. Beat constantly with an electric beater, whisk, or rotary beater for 7 minutes or until stiff, glossy peaks form. Remove from the heat and beat a few minutes more or until cool and of a spreadable consistency.

*ABOVE: Nothing can compare to this cake
made with freshly grated coconut.*

RASPBERRY PURÉE

MAKES 4 CUPS

*1 10-ounce package frozen
   raspberries, thawed*

*Sugar to taste
2 to 3 teaspoons kirsch*

Purée the ingredients in a food processor or blender until smooth. Strain through
a fine sieve. Keep it chilled until ready to serve.

A Celebration Dinner

*I*f you can find no reason to celebrate, invent one quickly and rely on this engaging menu to delight all co-celebrants. What to celebrate? Well, there's always a birthday, or, at this time of year, Easter, Mother's Day, St. Patrick's Day, and the day for the April Fools. But the real cause for celebration in springtime is spring itself: the rebirth of the green year, marked each year by the vernal equinox that falls on or about March 21. Every pagan society enjoyed its rites of spring at this turning point in the calendar. The Christian festival of Easter is itself an echo of these ancient revels, for it celebrates the Resurrection of Christ. In spring, optimism reveals itself out of thin air; the earth has roused itself and, inside, our cooking is transformed by the availability of fresh fruits and vegetables.

This celebration dinner is quite delicate. It is gracious and formal in feeling, though forthright and simple in its components. It takes advantage of what is fresh and abundant at the moment. Lightly stuffed veal medallions are bathed in a sauce of basil and lemon. Spectacular popovers house a filling of early spring mushrooms and garden peas. (Don't fear failure with the showy popovers. Just follow the recipe to the letter and success will be yours.) If you and your friends are addicted to strawberry shortcake in season, you may find yourselves equally enamored of the Paris-Brest, its luscious French equivalent.

M·e·n·u

GRATED BLACK AND RED
RADISHES
WITH SWEET BUTTER

·

ROLLED AND STUFFED
VEAL MEDALLIONS
WITH LEMON-BASIL SAUCE

·

GIANT POPOVERS

·

MORELS WITH SPRING PEAS

·

PARIS-BREST

ORDER OF PREPARATION

*A*s you probably want to make this a fancy party, you will want to do as much as possible ahead of time. The day before, you can bake the *pâte à choux* and make the pastry cream.

Select the meat carefully, because veal varies enormously in quality from coast to coast. Western veal is cut from a more mature calf; where possible, ask for eastern veal—white to light pink, never rosy, cut from the rib or loin.

A few hours before your guests arrive, wash and hull the strawberries, assemble the dessert, and refrigerate it. Mix the popover batter, cover, and set it aside. Pound the veal with a flat mallet (I dislike the spiked ones) and mix together the stuffing. Cook the morels and peas to the point of adding the cream and set them aside.

As friends arrive, start the popovers and finish the veal: Stuff the medallions, sauté them, and keep them warm in a low oven while you make the lemon-basil sauce. Add the cream to the morels and heat through. Serve each guest one giant popover filled with vegetables and two stuffed medallions of veal with some sauce. You might garnish each plate with sprigs of watercress. Make a big production of the dessert by placing long, thin French candles all around the top.

Wine suggestion: Choose an assertive Chardonnay with good acidity.

> "*I*t's that extra small thing on the plate, the fourth thing, that makes a meal memorable."
> **NORA EPHRON**

GRATED BLACK AND RED RADISHES WITH SWEET BUTTER

SERVES 6

10 to 12 small Flamboyant radishes (see Note) with leaves removed
10 to 12 small Spanish black radishes (see Note) with leaves removed
3 slices rye bread (preferably Oroweat European-style)
3 slices pumpernickel bread (preferably Oroweat European-style)
3 tablespoons unsalted butter, softened
Coarse salt

Coarsely grate the radishes. Trim the crusts from the breads and cut each slice into triangles. Spread the bread with the softened butter. Place a tablespoon or two of the grated black radish on top of the rye triangles and a tablespoon or two of the grated Flamboyant radish on the pumpernickel. Sprinkle with coarse salt. Serve immediately.

NOTE: The round, black Spanish radish, named for its black skin, takes a little longer than most radishes to mature. The Flamboyant radish, bright red with a white top, is a European variety about 2 inches long. Seeds for both are available from: Le Marche Seeds International, P.O. Box 566, Dixon, CA 95620.

Rolled and Stuffed Veal Medallions with Lemon-Basil Sauce

SERVES 6

12 thin veal medallions
(about 2 ounces each),
pounded flat
12 thin slices prosciutto
1 cup ricotta cheese
½ cup grated Provolone or
Gruyère cheese
2 tablespoons chopped fresh
basil, or 1 teaspoon dried
basil
1 tablespoon chopped fresh
oregano, or ½ teaspoon
dried oregano
1 tablespoon chopped fresh
thyme, or ½ teaspoon
dried thyme

½ cup cooked and chopped
spinach with all liquid
pressed out
All-purpose flour for
dusting
2 tablespoons unsalted
butter
2 tablespoons vegetable oil
Salt and freshly ground
black pepper to taste
Lemon-Basil Sauce (recipe
follows)
GARNISH
Whole fresh basil leaves

Cover each slice of pounded veal with 1 slice of prosciutto. In a bowl, mix together the cheeses, herbs, and spinach. Place approximately 2 tablespoons of this filling in the center of each slice of veal and roll up. Close the rolls securely with a toothpick, and dust with flour.

In a frying pan, heat the butter and oil. Sauté the veal medallions seam-side down in several batches until golden, about 5 to 7 minutes. Transfer to a warm serving platter and keep warm while you finish cooking the remaining veal rolls.

Serve each guest 2 medallions with some Lemon-Basil Sauce and garnish with additional whole fresh basil leaves.

Lemon-Basil Sauce

MAKES ABOUT 3 CUPS

1½ cups dry white wine
2 small shallots, minced
1 cup whole fresh basil
leaves
½ cup (1 stick) unsalted
butter

2 tablespoons freshly
squeezed lemon juice
Salt and freshly ground
black pepper to taste

In a medium-size saucepan, reduce the wine, shallots, and basil to ½ cup over high heat. Strain through a sieve lined with cheesecloth and return to the saucepan, which has been wiped clean. Whisk in the butter, one teaspoon at a time, over low heat; then stir in the lemon juice and season with salt and pepper. Reheat or keep warm over very low heat or in a *bain-marie* so the butter will not separate.

"There is no cure for birth and death, save to enjoy the interval."
GEORGE SANTAYANA

*ABOVE: A veal medallion with lemon-basil sauce and a giant popover
filled with morels and spring peas*

OPPOSITE: A Paris-Brest, ideal for any celebration

A fabulous and extremely simple recipe from that great cook, Julie Wagner. You will need a standard popover pan.

GIANT POPOVERS

SERVES 6

6 tablespoons unsalted butter,
  melted
2 cups all-purpose flour
1 teaspoon salt

6 jumbo or extra-large eggs
2 cups milk
Morels with Spring Peas
  (recipe follows)

Preheat the oven to 375° F. Paint the inside of the popover cups with a little of the melted butter.

Combine the flour and salt in a bowl. Beat the eggs just to mix and add to the flour along with the milk and remaining melted butter. Beat just to mix. Pour into the greased popover cups and bake for 50 to 60 minutes. Cut a slit in the top of each popover during the last 5 minutes of baking to allow steam to escape.

Pull the popovers in half and spoon the vegetable mixture into the bottom halves. Replace the tops, slightly askew, and serve immediately.

MORELS WITH SPRING PEAS

SERVES 6

1 pound fresh morels with
  stems removed, cleaned
4 tablespoons unsalted
  butter
½ cup Amontillado sherry

1 pound fresh peas, shelled
2 cups heavy cream
  Salt and freshly ground
  black pepper to taste

If the morels are very large, cut them in half lengthwise.

Melt the butter in a large skillet and sauté the mushrooms over high heat until tender, about 8 to 10 minutes. Add 2 tablespoons of the sherry and the peas and cook 3 minutes more. Remove to a bowl. Add the remaining sherry to the pan and cook over high heat until it is reduced to a few thick tablespoons. Add the cream and reduce to half over low heat. Return the morels and peas to the sauce and season with salt and pepper.

●   ·   ●   ·   ●   ·   ●   ·   ☙   ·   ●   ·   ●   ·   ●   ·   ●

A close cousin of the monstrous popovers, this is an oversize ring-shaped éclair filled with an almond-flavored cream and served with fresh strawberries heaped in the center. A French variation on the all-American strawberry shortcake.

PARIS-BREST

SERVES 6

PÂTE À CHOUX

6 tablespoons unsalted butter,
  cut into small pieces
1 cup boiling water
1 teaspoon granulated sugar
  Pinch of salt
1 cup all-purpose flour, sifted
4 large eggs, beaten

1 egg beaten with 1
  tablespoon water
2 pints strawberries, hulled
  and washed
  Confectioners' sugar
  (optional)

PASTRY CREAM

6 large egg yolks at room
   temperature
1 cup sugar
   Pinch of salt
½ cup all-purpose flour
3 cups milk, scalded

3 tablespoons unsalted
   butter, cut into small
   pieces
1 teaspoon almond extract
2 teaspoons vanilla extract

Preheat the oven to 425° F. Lightly oil and flour a baking sheet or line it with parchment paper.

Prepare the pâte à choux. In a medium-size saucepan, combine the butter, boiling water, sugar, and salt. Stir over low heat until the butter melts. Remove from the heat. Add the flour, all at once, and beat vigorously with a wooden spoon until well blended and the mixture pulls away from the sides of the pan. Beat the eggs thoroughly into the mixture, one at a time. Continue beating a few extra moments after the last egg has been added to make sure it is well blended.

Fill a large pastry bag fitted with the largest plain tip or no tip at all, and pipe the choux paste onto the prepared baking sheet in two wide overlapping ring shapes, 9 inches in diameter and 1½ inches thick. If it looks a little uneven, don't worry; it will come together during the baking. Brush the top and sides with the egg wash and bake for 20 minutes. Remove from the oven and, with a sharp knife or skewer, pierce the pastry in several spots around its middle. Lower the oven temperature to 325° F. and continue baking for 10 minutes more or until golden.

Remove from the oven and, while the pastry is still hot, use a serrated knife to cut it in half horizontally, making the bottom slightly deeper than the top.

Gently pull any uncooked, moist dough from the inside of both halves and discard. Let the pastry cool completely on a wire rack. Place the two halves together gently, loosely wrap the ring in plastic wrap, and store at room temperature overnight.

To prepare the pastry cream, beat the egg yolks until pale in a mixing bowl. Gradually add the sugar and beat until slightly thick. Beat in the salt and flour. Add the boiling milk little by little and stir. Pour into a saucepan and cook over medium heat until thick, stirring constantly and making sure the spoon reaches all the edges of the pan. Remove from the heat and add the butter in small pieces. Stir in the flavorings. Cool completely, cover with plastic wrap, and refrigerate.

To assemble the Paris-Brest, place the bottom half of the choux pastry on a round platter. Spoon the cream into the shell and center the top half over it. Fill the center of the ring with the strawberries and, if you wish, dust with confectioners' sugar just before serving. The dessert may be assembled an hour or so before serving and refrigerated without getting soggy.

"The year's at the Spring and day's at the morn."
ROBERT BROWNING

A Visual Feast

OPPOSITE: Contrasting textures and rich flavors, three-colored pasta with slivers of lobster

*T*his whole dinner has less than 700 calories per person, but it is so visually pleasing, so enlivened by fresh and surprising combinations, colors, and textures, that you won't miss the calories. This is the essence of "spa" cuisine: moderation made easier by the skillful play of aesthetics. Actually, spa cuisine is not really new. Early contributors to the notion of eating healthily and well without resorting to bean sprouts, wheat germ, or pallid hospital food include Adele Davis, J. I. Rodale, and French chef Michel Guérard, who championed the art of *cuisine minceur*. There *is* something about food that has come to the table in as near as possible a natural condition that is especially ravishing to the eye.

Spring is a good time to try this dinner. Ingredients at their crispest and brightest are available from local gardens, and it is easier to eat less in this season. Our sensory appetites, often focused on food all winter long, are satisfied on so many other levels when we are confronted with all the sights, sounds, and smells of a reawakened natural world. This dinner is not "diet" food. All of it—from the salmon and caviar to the chocolate mousse—is very good and also elegant. Yes, it is food that is nutritious, low in both calories and fat, but, more important, it is fresh, simple, and delicious. But let me caution you: Don't make extra. This way you won't be tempted to have a little more.

M·e·n·u

SMOKED SALMON PIZZAS
WITH GOLDEN CAVIAR

·

THREE-COLORED PASTA
WITH LOBSTER
AND LEMON-TARRAGON SAUCE

·

TENDER LEAF SALAD
WITH GRAPEFRUIT
VINAIGRETTE

·

SPA CHOCOLATE MOUSSE

ORDER OF PREPARATION

*T*his menu requires some last-minute work in the kitchen. Things will look their best if you work this way, but, bear in mind, activity burns calories. Schedule your time by shopping and setting the table early so you can prepare for dinner in the hour or so before your guests arrive.

Make the chocolate mousse and keep it well chilled in individual glasses. Wash the salad greens, section the grapefruit, and slice the mushrooms. Assemble the salad and refrigerate it. Then make the vinaigrette and set it aside.

Make the sauce for the pasta and slice the carrots and zucchini. Start boiling the water. Char the tortillas and assemble the ''pizzas'' as the guests arrive. After the first course, duck back into the kitchen and finish the pasta and toss the salad. Serve the refreshing dessert with an almond- or cinnamon-flavored coffee.

Wine suggestion: Serve the stylish, full-bodied Chardonnay.

*C*harred flour tortillas are the base for these quick-to-prepare ''pizzas.''

SMOKED SALMON PIZZAS WITH GOLDEN CAVIAR

SERVES 6

6 6-inch flour tortillas
½ cup plain yogurt
¼ cup sour cream
1 tablespoon chopped fresh
  chives

6 ounces smoked salmon,
  sliced paper-thin
6 dill sprigs
2 tablespoons golden caviar

Toast the flour tortillas on both sides for a few seconds over the open flame of a gas range or warm them in a 350° F. oven for 4 to 5 minutes, turning once.

Combine the yogurt, sour cream, and chives in a bowl. Spread each tortilla with 1½ to 2 tablespoons of the sauce; then top with 1 ounce of smoked salmon, a dill sprig, and 1 teaspoon of golden caviar. Serve at once.

''*H*ow long does getting thin take?' Pooh asked anxiously.''
A. A. MILNE

THREE-COLORED PASTA WITH LOBSTER AND LEMON-TARRAGON SAUCE

SERVES 6

1 cup dry white wine
2 tablespoons minced shallots
1 bunch fresh tarragon with stems
2 tablespoons unsalted butter
1 teaspoon arrowroot
2 tablespoons freshly squeezed lemon juice
Salt and freshly ground pepper to taste
2 small carrots, peeled

2 medium-size zucchini
1/4 pound spinach linguine or egg noodles
1/4 pound tomato linguine or egg noodles
1/4 pound egg linguine or egg noodles
12 ounces cooked lobster meat, torn into bite-size pieces

GARNISH
Chopped fresh tarragon leaves or chives

There is a trick to this that I learned from the Sonoma Mission Inn. Create a trompe-l'oeil effect of abundance by cutting the vegetables the same size and shape as the pasta. It not only looks filling, but feels that way, too.

Combine the wine, shallots, and half of the tarragon, stems and all, in a medium-size saucepan and reduce by half over high heat. Strain through a sieve lined with cheesecloth and return to the same saucepan, which has been wiped clean. Over low heat whisk in the butter a little at a time. Dissolve the arrowroot in the lemon juice and add it to the sauce. Simmer gently for 2 minutes or until thickened. Add the remaining tarragon leaves, finely chopped, and season with salt and pepper. Set aside.

Bring 4 quarts of salted water to a boil. Cut the carrots and zucchini into thin ribbonlike strips, about the same thickness as the pasta. You may do this by hand or with the thin slicing blade of the food processor. Put the carrots and zucchini into a large strainer and blanch them for a few seconds in the boiling water. Rinse immediately under cold water, drain, and pat dry. Cook the pasta in the same boiling water until al dente. Drain and refresh under cold water.

In a large saucepan or skillet, combine the pasta, blanched vegetables, lobster, and sauce over low heat and heat thoroughly, tossing gently to prevent sticking. Divide among 6 heated dinner plates and top with a sprinkling of tarragon or chives.

NEVER TOO THIN. I give you the great gastronome Brillat-Savarin on diet. He runs on a bit, but don't we all. "Be reassured, I shall map out a diet for you, and prove to you that there are still a few pleasures left for you here on this earth where we live to eat. . . . Every summer you must drink thirty bottles of Seltzer water, a big glass in the morning, two before luncheon and two more on going to bed. In general, drink white wines, light and acidulous ones like those of Anjou. Shun beer as if it were the plague, and eat often of radishes, fresh artichokes with a simple dressing, asparagus, celery, and cardoons. Among meats choose veal and poultry; eat only the crust of bread. . . . Any antifat diet should be accompanied by a precaution which I should have mentioned at the very beginning: it consists of wearing day and night a belt which supports the belly at the same time that it moderately confines it. . . . The belt also acts as a warning sentinel by feeling uncomfortable when one has eaten too much. . . ."

A smoked salmon pizza crowned with caviar

A light, quenching spritzer

Scooped again: a surprisingly low-in-calorie chocolate mousse

Combine your own mixture of tender spring greens—arugula, dandelion greens, mache, watercress, lamb's-quarters, nasturtium, and spinach—whatever is available.

TENDER LEAF SALAD WITH GRAPEFRUIT VINAIGRETTE

SERVES 6

VINAIGRETTE
- ½ teaspoon minced garlic
- 1 tablespoon grainy-type Dijon mustard
- 2 tablespoons chopped chives
- 1 teaspoon finely chopped fresh basil
- 1 teaspoon finely chopped fresh oregano
- tablespoons safflower or 2 olive oil
- ¼ cup freshly squeezed grapefruit juice

- 2 tablespoons sparkling mineral water
- Salt and freshly ground black pepper to taste

- 1 pound tender leaves, washed, stemmed, and drained
- 2 cups thinly sliced fresh mushrooms
- 2 pink grapefruit, peeled and sectioned

Combine all the ingredients for the vinaigrette in a jar or blender and shake well or blend to mix thoroughly. Chill until ready to use.

When ready to serve, gently toss together in a large bowl the leaves, mushrooms, grapefruit sections, and dressing and divide among individual salad plates.

Terry Richards, the nutritionist at the Sonoma Mission Inn, contributed this delicious, rich-tasting mousse with only 25 to 30 calories per serving. The substitution of sugar for the Equal makes a dessert portion of about 45 calories.

SPA CHOCOLATE MOUSSE

SERVES 6 TO 8

- 1½ cups nonfat skim milk
- 6 packages Equal sweetener or 3 tablespoons sugar
- 4 tablespoons unsweetened dark cocoa powder

- 2 to 3 drops orange extract
GARNISH
- Grated orange rind or whole strawberries

Blend all the ingredients thoroughly using an immersion blender (see Note). Spoon the mousse into 6 well-chilled dessert cups or long-stemmed glasses and top each with orange zest or a fresh strawberry.

NOTE: The immersion blender is a small, hand-held blender capable of whipping nonfat skim milk to the consistency of whipped cream. The skim milk may be flavored with a variety of extracts and a low-calorie sweetener and then piled high on fresh fruit or other desserts, adding only 4 calories per tablespoon. Look for Taurus or Braun brands available in major department stores, cookware stores, and cookware catalogues. It is also available by mail order, from: Sonoma Mission Inn, attention Retail Manager, P.O. Box 1447, Sonoma, CA 95476.

High on the Hog

M·e·n·u

LACY POTATO PANCAKES

·

BAKED HAM
WITH APRICOT-MUSTARD GLAZE

·

PINEAPPLE CHUTNEY

·

BELGIAN ENDIVE
AND TOMATO AU GRATIN

·

LIME CHEESECAKE

*L*ike a good man or true love, a good ham is hard to find. And that's too bad, because at Easter what you want is something outstanding, with superior flavor, glorious for a celebration, memorable. Obviously a bad ham won't do. You know the ones: the boneless canned hams spurting water and so spiked with liquid smoke you might as well be eating a fireman's hat. But there *are* good hams —those smoky, russet, flavor-loaded beauties from the South where, according to Bill Neal in his delightful book *Bill Neal's Southern Cooking,* pork was long the favorite and staple meat, considered vastly more nutritious than beef. Baked ham at Easter is an all-American custom, as traditional here as lamb in Greece and hot-crossed buns in England. We should revel in it, especially during this period of the rediscovery of our country's great regional foods.

This menu is for a stylish red-white-and-blue Easter. The ham is the "good" kind, the accompaniments updated: lacy potato pancakes, endive and tomatoes au gratin, pineapple chutney (the pineapple is in the chutney this time out, not molded ring by ring from the can to the top of the ham). Cheesecake—alas, the kind of thing one wants *all* the time—is a dessert often associated with feasting and with Easter. This is the excuse you've been waiting for.

*T*he real McCoy. I think success with ham depends as much on the selection of a good-quality ham as on any recipe. See the notes on page 44 for buying suggestions.

ORDER OF PREPARATION

*T*he chutney and the cheesecake can be made a day ahead. This gives the flavors of the chutney a chance to meld together and the cheesecake a chance to chill.

Prepare the endive and tomato au gratin either while the ham is cooking or ahead of time and warm it in the same oven. Decide before baking the ham if you wish to serve it warm or at room temperature. Let it "rest" at least 10 minutes before carving. While the ham is in the oven, make the potato pancakes and keep them warm in a low oven.

You can serve the dinner buffet style or sit down. Put one person in charge of carving the ham. Serve the lime cheesecake well chilled and cut into thin wedges.

Wine suggestion: Offer a crisp and lively Zinfandel.

LACY POTATO PANCAKES

SERVES 6

2 large eggs, beaten
½ cup all-purpose flour
½ teaspoon salt
¼ cup beer
¼ cup finely chopped scallions, white part only

2 baking potatoes, peeled and kept in cold water until ready to use
Vegetable oil for frying

In a large bowl, mix together the eggs, flour, salt, beer, and scallions. Set aside.

Using the julienne blade of the food processor, finely grate (or julienne) the potatoes. Squeeze out any moisture and add the potatoes to the batter. Blend well and, using wet hands, form 2½-inch loosely packed pancakes. As you make them, drop them into a skillet containing ½ inch of hot vegetable oil. Fry for 3 to 4 minutes on each side or until golden brown. You will have to do this in batches. Drain the pancakes on paper towels and keep them warm in a low oven until ready to serve.

BAKED HAM WITH APRICOT-MUSTARD GLAZE

SERVES 6

1 10- to 12-pound fully cooked bone-in smoked ham
Whole cloves to decorate
½ cup Dijon mustard

4 garlic cloves, smashed and peeled
⅓ cup apricot jam
2 tablespoons orange juice
½ cup firmly packed dark brown sugar

Preheat the oven to 375° F. Line a large roasting pan with aluminum foil. With a sharp knife score the top of the ham in a grid pattern about ¼ inch deep. Stud the bone end with cloves. Put the ham into the prepared pan.

Combine the remaining ingredients in a bowl and blend into a smooth sauce. Spread the glaze evenly over the top and sides of the ham. Bake for 45 minutes to 1 hour, basting several times. Serve warm or at room temperature.

A perfect Easter dinner:
apricot-glazed baked ham, lacy potato
pancakes, and pineapple chutney

MAIL-ORDER HAMS FROM AROUND THE COUNTRY. If you don't like what you see in your neighborhood, try one of these:

Blew Farms, Oakgrove Plantation, R.R. 2, Box 255, Pittstown, NJ 08867; (201) 782-9618. Average weight 14 to 16 pounds; hickory smoked for 2 weeks.

Meadow Farms Country Smokehouse, P.O. Box 1387, Bishop, CA 93514; (619) 873-5311. Average weight 18 to 22 pounds; no sodium nitrate or other preservatives.

Ozark Mountain Smokehouse, P.O. Box 37, Farmington, AR 72730; (800) 643-3437. Average weight 14 to 15 pounds; hickory and sassafras smoked.

Harrington's in Vermont, Richmond, VT 05477; (802) 434-3411. Average weight 13 pounds; cob smoked.

*B*elgian endive, crisp and piquant, cuts the rich taste of the ham.

PINEAPPLE CHUTNEY

SERVES 6

1 large ripe pineapple with "eyes" removed, peeled and cut into 1-inch cubes
3 medium-size onions, peeled
1 sweet green pepper, seeded and cut into 1-inch cubes
1 sweet red pepper, seeded and cut into 1-inch cubes
3 garlic cloves, peeled and minced
¾ cup packed light brown sugar
¾ cup cider vinegar

½ cup golden raisins
½ cup dried currants
¼ cup peeled and chopped fresh ginger
1 teaspoon salt
2 cinnamon sticks, broken in half
1 teaspoon dark mustard seeds
½ teaspoon coriander seeds
¼ teaspoon whole black peppercorns
½ teaspoon whole cloves
2 small dried chile peppers

Mix together the chopped pineapple, onions, peppers, garlic, sugar, and vinegar in a large noncorrodible pot. Cook, stirring frequently, until the mixture is thick, about 30 minutes. Add the raisins, currants, ginger, and salt. Tie the cinnamon sticks, mustard and coriander seeds, peppercorns, cloves, and chile peppers in a square of cheesecloth and add to the chutney. Bring to a boil and simmer for 30 minutes more or until the liquid becomes thick and syrupy. Cool, cover, and refrigerate. This chutney will keep for up to a week in the refrigerator.

BELGIAN ENDIVE AND TOMATO AU GRATIN

SERVES 6

10 to 12 plump heads endive, trimmed
2 tablespoons freshly squeezed lemon juice
1 teaspoon sugar
2 tablespoons unsalted butter

SAUCE
3 slices bacon
½ small onion, finely chopped
2 garlic cloves, peeled and minced
¼ cup peeled and finely chopped carrot

½ cup dry white wine
⅛ teaspoon crushed red pepper
1 1-pound can plum tomatoes, drained and chopped
1 tablespoon fresh basil, or ½ teaspoon dried basil
Salt and freshly ground black pepper to taste
¼ cup pitted black olives

GARNISH
Chopped fresh parsley

Place the endive in a saucepan with enough boiling water to cover. Add the lemon juice and sugar. Cover and simmer until the outer leaves are tender and the inside is still crisp, about 10 minutes. Drain well. Melt the butter in a skillet. Add the drained endive and brown on all sides.

Preheat the oven to 375° F. Butter a shallow gratin or baking dish.

Fry the bacon until crisp and reserve 2 tablespoons of the fat. Reserve the bacon for another use. Add the onion, garlic, and carrot to the bacon fat and simmer until the vegetables are just soft. Add the wine, crushed red pepper, tomatoes, and basil and season generously with salt and pepper. Simmer until the sauce is reduced to a moist purée.

Pour the sauce into the prepared dish. Drain the endive and place it on top of the sauce. (Devotees of the crunchy-topped casserole can scatter breadcrumbs mixed with Parmesan cheese over all.) Bake for 15 minutes. Five minutes before serving, arrange the black olives in the tomato sauce. Garnish with the parsley.

LIME CHEESECAKE

SERVES 6 TO 8

A light cheesecake, quick and easy to prepare.

2 cups crushed Carr's
  Wheatmeal Biscuits, or
  graham crackers
2/3 cup unsalted butter,
  melted
1 8-ounce package cream
  cheese, softened
2 large eggs, beaten

1 14-ounce can sweetened
  condensed milk
Grated rind of 1 lime
Juice of 2 limes
GARNISH
  Paper-thin lime slices
  dipped in granulated
  sugar

Preheat the oven to 350° F.

Combine the biscuit crumbs and melted butter. Press the mixture evenly over the sides and bottom of a 9-inch tart pan with a removable rim. Bake for 8 to 10 minutes. Cool on a wire rack.

In a bowl, beat together the cream cheese, eggs, condensed milk, and lime rind and juice until smooth. Pour into the prepared crust and bake for 25 to 30 minutes or until set. Cool on a wire rack; then remove the rim of the pan and chill the cheesecake. Serve decorated with paper-thin lime slices dipped in granulated sugar.

LEFTOVER HAM TO KILL. Dorothy Parker is supposed to have once described eternity as two people and a ham. But don't worry about leftover ham. If you think you have more leftovers than late-night refrigerator-to-mouth predators can polish off in a day or two, freeze a good quantity of the cooked ham (this works very well) and serve it later with spring vegetables when the appetite for ham has reasserted itself.

Salad Daze

A spring dinner built around the salad principle is a natural, perfectly suited to the fine seasonal intoxication and first welcome blast of warm weather. "We'll just have a big salad," you say, and for the first time this sounds like a good idea rather than a dieter's last ditch *folie* in an attempt to turn the tide. Of course, salad does want some other things along with it and this menu has them, but salad alone (consider the ingenious "composed" salads that have now displaced the dreary lettuce-tomato-cucumber combination of yesteryear) is now an acceptable and satisfying main-dish alternative. The vast array of "discovered" salad ingredients is one of the glories of the "new" cuisine. Peruse the salad sections of ingredient-conscious menus and cookbooks and you will see that a whole new army of leafy and crunchy edibles has invaded the garden lexicon. (If you wonder, somewhat despairingly, "What *are* all these things?" you have lots of company.)

If you feel confident that a beautiful, fresh, delicately flavored salad of blanched spring vegetables with light accompaniments is enough for your guests, by all means forego the smoked chicken breast. Just use your judgment: You know best what your friends like. The main idea here is to keep it simple and to throw pretension and fussy elaboration out with the March winds.

M·e·n·u

ASPARAGUS SALAD JARDINIÈRE
WITH MAYONNAISE
AUX FINES HERBES

·

DEEP-FRIED CAMEMBERT
WITH WILD LINGONBERRY
PRESERVES

·

COLD SMOKED CHICKEN BREAST

·

AMARETTI-RHUBARB CRISP

OPPOSITE: *Salads—the easiest way to entertain*

ORDER OF PREPARATION

*T*his dinner makes no serious demands on the cook. Everything is simple and straightforward and can be made in the hour before your guests arrive.

Assemble and bake the Amaretti-rhubarb crisp first. While it is baking, shape the Camembert pastries and cover them with a damp towel. Make the mayonnaise and refrigerate it along with some white wine. Prepare the vegetables and bring the salted water to a boil. Boil the eggs, cook the carrots, and blanch the green vegetables. Make an appealing arrangement of the vegetables, garnish with the eggs, and cover with plastic wrap or a damp towel. Slice the poultry. Hold the salad and sliced poultry at room temperature.

As your guests arrive, heat the oil and fry the cheese pastries. Serve on small plates with the lingonberry preserves. Serve the salad and smoked chicken with some good bread and sweet butter. The delicate pink rhubarb crisp rounds out the dinner.

Wine suggestion: A rich full-bodied Cabernet Sauvignon nicely complements the Camembert cheese and smoked chicken breast.

*D*iana Vreeland, whose style is legend and who minces no words, says, "Asparagus should be sexy and almost fluid. . . ." This sounds about right.

"The first gathering of the garden in May of salads, radishes, and herbs made me feel like a mother about her baby—how could anything so beautiful be mine. And this emotion of wonder filled me for each vegetable as it was gathered every year. There is nothing that is comparable to it, as satisfactory or as thrilling, as gathering the vegetables one has grown."**

ALICE B. TOKLAS
The Alice B. Toklas Cookbook

ASPARAGUS SALAD JARDINIÈRE WITH MAYONNAISE AUX FINES HERBES

SERVES 6

2 pounds asparagus, peeled
    of tough outer scales,
    trimmed to even lengths,
    and tied into 6 bundles
1 pound green beans, tipped
    and tailed, trimmed to
    even lengths
1 pound baby carrots,
    peeled

1 tablespoon sugar
1 tablespoon unsalted butter
    Salt and freshly ground
    black pepper to taste
½ pound mushrooms, sliced
6 large eggs, hard boiled
    and cut in half
    Mayonnaise aux Fines
    Herbes (recipe follows)

Bring 4 to 5 quarts of salted water to a rapid boil in a large kettle. Gently drop the asparagus bundles into the boiling water and cover the pot. When the water begins to boil again, blanch the asparagus for 10 to 12 minutes or until the thick ends are just tender. Remove the bundles and immediately plunge them into a sink filled with ice water to stop the cooking. Drain, cover with a cloth, and keep at room temperature.

Blanch the green beans by the same method as the asparagus until just tender, 8 to 10 minutes. Plunge in the ice water. Drain, cover with a cloth, and keep at room temperature.

In a medium-size saucepan, combine the carrots with the sugar, butter, and 1 cup of water. Cover and bring to a simmer. Cook for 12 to 15 minutes or until the carrots are just tender and the water has evaporated. Season with salt and pepper and cool to room temperature.

Arrange the cooked vegetables on a large platter and garnish with sliced mushrooms, egg halves, and Mayonnaise aux Fines Herbes.

MAYONNAISE AUX FINES HERBES

MAKES 3 CUPS

1 teaspoon Dijon mustard
  Salt and freshly ground
  black pepper to taste
3 large egg yolks
1½ cups olive oil
2 teaspoons white wine
  vinegar
1 teaspoon honey

1 tablespoon finely chopped
  fresh parsley
1 tablespoon finely chopped
  fresh mint
1 tablespoon finely chopped
  fresh chervil (optional)
¼ cup finely chopped
  shallots

In a bowl, whisk together the mustard, salt and pepper, and egg yolks for 2 minutes. Add ½ cup of the oil drop by drop, whisking all the time until the mixture begins to thicken. Now add the remaining 1 cup of oil more quickly, whisking all the time. Thin the mayonnaise with the vinegar. Stir in the honey, herbs, and shallots. Allow 3 to 4 tablespoons of mayonnaise per person.

DEEP-FRIED CAMEMBERT WITH WILD LINGONBERRY PRESERVES

SERVES 6

12 sheets filo pastry
¼ cup (½ stick) unsalted
  butter, melted
12 ounces Camembert cheese,
  cut into 1-ounce pieces

Peanut oil for deep-frying
1 10-ounce jar wild
  lingonberry preserves

Lay the filo dough on a damp tea towel and cover with plastic wrap or another damp towel to keep it from drying out. Take one sheet of pastry at a time, and brush it generously all over with some of the melted butter. Place 1 ounce of the Camembert in the bottom corner and fold over the bottom end of the dough to make a triangle. Fold the triangle upward and continue folding up and over in exact triangles until you reach the top of the pastry. Repeat with the remaining cheese and pastry.

Deep-fry the pastry triangles in hot oil at least 2 inches deep until golden brown, about 1 minute. Remove and drain on paper towels. These can be reheated or kept warm in a low oven until ready to serve. Serve with a dollop of lingonberry preserves on each plate.

COLD SMOKED CHICKEN BREAST

SERVES 6

Thinly slice 6 cold smoked chicken breasts on the diagonal and arrange on a platter. Accompany with more Mayonnaise aux Fines Herbes, if desired.

NEW-FANGLED CONVENIENCE. Cold smoked poultry belongs to the new category of dressed-up convenience foods increasingly available from gourmet shops and good delicatessens. Smoked over alderwood with all natural ingredients, it comes fully cooked and ready for the table. Look for whole boneless chicken breasts (weighing about 8 ounces each), whole poussin (bone-in, 1½ to 2 pounds each), or whole breast of turkey (2 to 5 pounds each).

Sweet and sassy: a rhubarb crisp topped with a crunchy sprinkling of Amaretti cookies and, if you like, whipped cream flavored with Amaretto liqueur

AMARETTI-RHUBARB CRISP

SERVES 6 TO 8

3 pounds rhubarb (7 to 8 cups diced into ¹/₂-inch cubes)
1 cup golden raisins
¹/₄ cup Grand Marnier or Cointreau
¹/₂ cup granulated sugar
3 tablespoons cornstarch
Grated rind of 1 orange
12 Amaretti cookies (see Note), coarsely broken (2 cups)

1 cup rolled oats
¹/₄ cup packed dark brown sugar
2 teaspoons ground cinnamon
¹/₂ cup coarsely chopped almonds
³/₄ cup (1¹/₂ sticks) cold unsalted butter, cut into small pieces
1 large egg, beaten

Preheat the oven to 350° F. Generously butter a 3-quart shallow baking dish.

In a bowl, combine the rhubarb, raisins, Grand Marnier, granulated sugar, cornstarch, and orange rind. Pour into the prepared baking dish.

In a separate bowl, mix together the Amaretti cookies, rolled oats, dark brown sugar, cinnamon, and almonds. Work the butter in thoroughly with your fingers. Add the egg and stir just to bind. Sprinkle the topping evenly over the fruit mixture and bake for 45 to 50 minutes, or until the rhubarb is bubbling

NOTE: Look for Amaretti di Saronno in the bright red tins.

Pretty in Pink

*S*pring comes in colors, and two of its loveliest, pink and pale green, are highlighted in this menu. For pink, we have the rosy hue of fresh grilled salmon, the raspberry vinegar of the salad, the strawberry sauce for the angel food cake, and the pearly mauve skins of the new potatoes. Accompanying the salmon is a salad of juxtaposed greens—the dark green, fringed chicory and slices of palest green avocado.

This is a dinner tailored to complement the annual national rite of passage that, with the onset of warm weather, dictates the abandonment of the kitchen range for the grill and the dining room for the deck, backyard, or beach. The Indians of the Pacific Northwest liked to roast their salmon on tall ironwood stakes set over an open fire on the beach. This sounds like an incomparable way of preparing the fish—out of doors, perhaps in the light of a red sun sinking into the Pacific. We can approximate the effect by taking a beautiful whole fish and cooking it directly on a grill over a bed of hot glowing coals and aromatic wood chips. Don't even think about wrapping the fish in aluminum foil before you set it on the grill; if you do this, you might as well have baked it in the oven.

M·e·n·u

SUNBURST OF AVOCADO
ON A CHICORY CHIFFONADE
WITH ORANGE-GINGER VINAIGRETTE

·

GRILLED KING SALMON

·

TINY NEW POTATOES
WITH LEMON, CAPERS, GARLIC,
AND MINT

·

ARTICHOKE CHIPS

·

REUNION ANGEL CAKE
WITH FRESH STRAWBERRY SAUCE

ORDER OF PREPARATION

*A*lthough everything is best prepared on the day it is going to be eaten, you can marinate the fish the day ahead, and if you like, make the cake and its sauce, although angel food cake is really best the same day it is made.

A few hours before dinner, wash, dry, and refrigerate the chicory. Mix the vinaigrette and set it aside. Start the fire an hour before you wish to eat, allowing 30 minutes for the coals and wood chips to come to the proper temperature and 20 to 30 minutes for the grilling of the salmon. Begin cooking the potatoes just before you put the fish on the grill. Slice the Jerusalem artichoke chips, and pre-fry them, giving them their final fry and serving them hot from the oil sprinkled with salt as your guests arrive. While the salmon is cooking, finish cooking and then season the potatoes. Arrange the sunburst salad either on a large platter or on individual plates. Serve the light and airy reunion cake with the tangy strawberry sauce.

Wine suggestion: For this light, simple meal, try an attractive, light, and fruity Pinot Noir.

"**N**ature's first green is gold, Her hardest hue to hold, Her early leaf's a flower; But only so an hour. Then leaf subsides to leaf, So Eden sank to grief, So dawn goes down to day, Nothing gold can stay."
ROBERT FROST

SUNBURST OF AVOCADO ON A CHICORY CHIFFONADE WITH ORANGE-GINGER VINAIGRETTE

SERVES 6

VINAIGRETTE
- 1 garlic clove, peeled and minced
- 1 tablespoon minced shallot
- 1 tablespoon peeled and minced fresh ginger
- 1 teaspoon Dijon mustard
- 1 orange, peeled, seeded, and sectioned
- Salt and freshly ground black pepper to taste

- 1/4 cup raspberry vinegar
- 1/2 cup olive oil
- 2 tablespoons vegetable oil

- 2 heads chicory or curly endive
- 2 large ripe avocados, peeled
- Juice of 2 lemons

GARNISH
- Coarsely chopped basil leaves

To make the Orange-Ginger Vinaigrette, in a food processor or blender, purée the garlic, shallots, ginger, mustard, and orange. Add the salt and pepper and vinegar and then the oils, processing until the dressing is smooth.

Chop the root off the base of each head of chicory or endive and wash each head well under cold running water. Dry completely and cut into thin strips.

Slice the avocados into 1/8-inch-thick slices and squeeze the lemon juice over them to prevent discoloration. Place the chiffonade of chicory on individual serving plates, arrange the avocado slices in a sunburst pattern around the chicory, drizzle a little dressing over each, and garnish with the chopped basil leaves.

GRILLED KING SALMON

SERVES 6

1 7- to 8-pound whole
   salmon, cleaned with head
   and tail left on, rib cage
   removed

MARINADE
2 tablespoons unsalted
   butter, melted
¼ cup freshly squeezed
   lemon juice
¼ cup soy sauce

1 medium-size onion,
   minced
¼ cup minced fresh parsley
¼ cup minced fresh
   coriander

GARNISH
Lemon wedges
Chopped fresh parsley or
   coriander

Rinse the salmon thoroughly under cold water; then pat it dry. Place the salmon in a noncorrodible baking dish or roasting pan. Combine the marinade ingredients in a bowl and pour over the fish. Cover and marinate in the refrigerator for several hours, or overnight, turning at least once.

Place the salmon on a clean oiled grill over a moderately hot fire and cover, using any large lid or make a cover from aluminum foil. If you see a lot of flame, the fire is too hot. Grill the fish for 10 to 12 minutes on the first side. Very, very carefully, using two large spatulas, turn the fish and grill for another 10 to 12 minutes or until a skewer or fork easily pierces the meat. Gently transfer the fish to a serving platter. Garnish with lemon wedges and chopped parsley or coriander.

TINY NEW POTATOES
WITH LEMON, CAPERS, GARLIC, AND MINT

SERVES 6

12 red new potatoes, as small
   as possible
Grated rind of 1 lemon
2 tablespoons drained capers
3 garlic cloves, peeled and
   minced
¼ cup chopped fresh mint

1 tablespoon coarse salt
¼ cup olive oil
2 tablespoons freshly
   squeezed lemon juice
Freshly ground black
   pepper to taste

Remove a cummerbund or spiral of skin from each potato with a small, sharp knife. Cook the potatoes in 4 quarts of salted boiling water until just tender, 20 to 30 minutes. Drain.

Combine the grated lemon rind, capers, garlic, mint, and salt in a bowl. In a large skillet, heat the oil. Add the potatoes and sauté them until they are golden brown. Add the lemon juice and lemon rind mixture, and toss well. Season with the pepper.

TIPS ON GRILLING FISH. When grilling fish directly over a hot fire, remember that rich and oily fish, such as salmon, tuna, or bluefish, handle better and are less likely to dry out than more flaky-fleshed fish, such as perch or flounder. For salmon, the Indians of the Pacific Northwest preferred a wood fire of alderwood and cherry—wonderful woods for this delectable fish. You can use a mix of charcoal briquets and wood chips.

To prevent sticking, make sure the grill is well cleaned, oiled, and hot. Have a glowing, but not a flaming fire: Too cold a fire encourages sticking. Be gentle when you turn the fish; don't be tempted to move it around a lot. Do not overcook it; remember that, like meat, it will continue to cook after it has come off the grill.

A glamorous King salmon followed by an old-fashioned angel food cake with a luscious strawberry sauce

ARTICHOKE CHIPS

SERVES 6

1½ pounds Jerusalem
    artichokes, peeled

Peanut oil for frying
Sea salt to taste

Slice the Jerusalem artichokes into chips as thinly as possible. Rinse the "chips" under cold water and pat them dry. Deep-fry them in several batches in hot, but not smoking, oil in a skillet until a pale golden color. Drain. Change the oil and briefly fry them again to a crisp golden brown. Drain each completed batch on a baking sheet lined with paper towels and keep warm in a low oven while you finish the remaining chips. Season generously with sea salt and serve immediately.

*S*ubtly flavored chips made from the Jerusalem artichoke.

REUNION ANGEL CAKE
WITH FRESH STRAWBERRY SAUCE

SERVES 6 TO 8

1 cup cake flour
1¼ cups egg whites (from 8
    to 9 large eggs) at room
    temperature
¼ teaspoon salt
1 teaspoon cream of tartar

1 teaspoon almond extract
1 teaspoon vanilla extract
1½ cups superfine sugar
    Fresh Strawberry Sauce
    (recipe follows)

Preheat the oven to 325° F.

Sift the cake flour, measure one cup, and sift twice more.

Beat the egg whites until frothy, sprinkle in the salt, cream of tartar, and flavorings and continue beating until stiff but not dry. Gradually fold in the sugar, 2 tablespoons at a time. Using a whisk, gradually fold in the flour. Turn into a well-washed and dried 9-inch *ungreased* tube or angel cake pan and bake for 1 hour. Remove from the oven and cool for 10 minutes on a wire rack. Run a knife around the edge of the pan, invert the pan onto a wire rack, and let the cake stand in the inverted pan for about 1 hour or until completely cooled. Remove from the pan. Serve with Fresh Strawberry Sauce.

FRESH STRAWBERRY SAUCE

MAKES 2 CUPS

1 pint fresh ripe
    strawberries, washed and
    hulled
⅓ cup sugar

¼ teaspoon almond extract
1 tablespoon Amaretto
    liqueur

Purée the strawberries in a food processor or blender until smooth. Strain into a bowl through a sieve lined with cheesecloth to remove the seeds. Combine the purée with the remaining ingredients, cover, and chill.

*T*his is the classic angel food cake that often makes appearances at old-style family gatherings across the country. The secret of its height and lightness lies in the volume of the egg whites.

Trout
Fishing
in
America

*F*ishing for your supper is a much-loved American pastime. A Memorial Day picnic right on the spot where the fish are caught can be an idyllic way to get friends and family out of doors for the big holiday. Of course it's not always a simple matter to get to a secluded spot all your own where the fish are biting, but a wonderful and *reliable* day's outing can be made to one of the country's well-stocked trout farms where, if you are lucky, your party will be supplied not only with bait and tackle but cooking facilities as well. At the trout farm we visited to photograph this menu (Smith's Mt. St. Helena Trout Farm and Hatchery, 18401 Ida Clayton Road, Calistoga, CA 94515; 707-987-3651), they cleaned the pretty 8- to 10-ounce rainbow trout for us —and we only paid for what we caught.

So pack up this picnic and go fishing. There is just enough activity for children, older participants are just as enthusiastic as younger ones, and all fishermen get caught up in the satisfying business of landing their own dinner. If lethargy and disorganization have you in their grip over the holiday (always perfectly understandable), you can sneak down to the fish market, buy some trout and, assured of your "catch," fire up the grill and picnic in fine style in the backyard.

ORDER OF PREPARATION

*W*hen planning the menu for a picnic, always take into account the fact that food must be easily transportable and "hold up" well. Consider what can be done in advance and what is to be cooked on the spot. You want to minimize the amount of equipment and ingredients carried to the site.

As you can surmise from its name, the earthquake cake emerges from the oven in a dilapidated condition and no long-distance transport can further corrode its cracked face—it is an excellent traveler. Prepare it at home, as much as several days in advance. The same is true for the sauce tartar.

Start the cracked wheat salad a day ahead. On the day of the outing finish it and put it in the refrigerator to chill. Assemble and skewer the *amuse gueules* and wrap them securely in aluminum foil. The fish, of course, is cooked from start to finish on the grill. Remember that people have more of an appetite and eat more out of doors, so estimate generous quantities of everything.

Wine suggestion: A crisp Sauvignon Blanc adds a touch of spice and herb to the grilled trout.

AMUSE GUEULES

Peeled garlic cloves	*Pitted Spanish olives,*
Whole tiny mushrooms	*stuffed with blanched*
	almonds (see Note)
	Thinly sliced bacon

*F*un little bites to eat while waiting for the main course. By wrapping everything in bacon, you keep the tidbits from drying out over the hot coals. Complement the *amuse gueules* with slices of grilled French bread and some crunchy, ice-cold julienned vegetables.

Wrap each garlic clove, mushroom, or stuffed Spanish olive in half a slice of bacon. Thread 3 or 4 onto a skewer. If you are using bamboo skewers, make sure to soak them first in water for 30 minutes. Place directly on the grill and grill for 4 to 5 minutes, turning once, or until bacon is crisp.

NOTE: Spanish olives stuffed with blanched almonds are available in the deli sections of most large grocery stores.

GRILLED WHOLE SCALLIONS

SERVES 6

12 scallions, washed and	*Olive oil*
trimmed	

Paint the scallions with the olive oil and grill, turning frequently until charred and just tender.

"*T*hey did not know that the quicker a fresh water fish is on the fire after it is caught, the better it is; and they reflected little upon what a sauce open-air sleeping, open-air exercise, bathing, and a large ingredient of hunger make for."

MARK TWAIN
By the Camp Fire

Grilled dilly trout with amuse gueules

Two of the world's greatest fishermen

The earthquake cake will please even the most passionate chocolate lovers

A dinner of freshly caught trout is one of the most delicate of eating experiences. The fish are best cooked very simply and quickly on the grill.

GRILLED DILLY TROUT

SERVES 6

12 to 18 small fresh trout (about 8 to 12 ounces each), cleaned with heads and tails left on
¼ cup olive oil
1 large bunch fresh dill

1 small onion, cut into thin slices and separated into rings
Salt and freshly ground black pepper to taste
GARNISH
Lemon wedges

Score the trout twice on each side and brush them with olive oil. Stuff the cavity of each fish with a small branch of dill and several onion rings. Season the skin with salt and pepper. Cook the fish fairly fast over a moderate fire, about 5 to 7 minutes on each side. Serve them garnished with lemon wedges.

SAUCE TARTAR

MAKES 2 CUPS

2 large eggs, hard-boiled, yolks separated from whites
1 tablespoon Dijon mustard
1 large egg yolk at room temperature
½ cup olive oil
2 teaspoons white wine vinegar
Salt and freshly ground black pepper to taste

2 tablespoons finely chopped fresh parsley
2 tablespoons finely chopped gherkin pickles
1 tablespoon drained capers
½ teaspoon grated lemon rind
2 tablespoons chopped fresh dill

In a bowl, mash the hard-boiled egg yolks to a paste with the mustard. Stir in the raw egg yolk. Beat in the olive oil drop by drop to make a mayonnaise, adding the drops of oil more quickly as the sauce thickens. Thin with the vinegar and season with salt and pepper. Finely chop the hard-boiled egg whites and stir them into the sauce along with the remaining ingredients. Cover and chill. Keeps one week in the refrigerator.

CRACKED WHEAT SALAD

SERVES 6

1 cup medium or fine
  bulgur
2/3 cup olive oil
2/3 cup freshly squeezed
  lemon juice
1 cucumber, peeled, seeded,
  and finely chopped
  (1 cup)
1 small green pepper, peeled,
  seeded, and finely chopped
  (1/2 cup)

1/2 cup finely chopped
  scallions, including some
  of the green ends
1 cup finely chopped fresh
  parsley
1/2 cup finely chopped fresh
  mint
GARNISH
  Cherry tomatoes
  Romaine lettuce leaves

Soak the bulgur at room temperature in the olive oil and lemon juice in a covered bowl overnight. Combine with the remaining ingredients and toss. Cover and chill the salad for at least an hour. Garnish with cherry tomatoes and lettuce leaves.

This is the refreshing Middle Eastern tabooleh made with bulgur (cracked wheat). No need to soak the grain in water or cook it; just remember to marinate it overnight in oil and lemon.

SAN FRANCISCO EARTHQUAKE CAKE

SERVES 6 TO 8

24 ounces semisweet
  chocolate, broken into
  small pieces
1 cup (2 sticks) unsalted
  butter

8 large eggs, at room
  temperature
3 cups confectioners' sugar,
  sifted
1/2 cup potato starch

Preheat the oven to 350° F. Grease an 8-inch springform pan and line the bottom with wax paper. Butter the wax paper and lightly dust the inside of the pan with flour.

Melt the chocolate and butter in the top of a covered double boiler over simmering water. Cool.

In a large bowl, beat the eggs until pale and thick and heavy ribbons form when the beaters are lifted. Fold in the cooled chocolate mixture and then the confectioners' sugar. Then sift and fold in the potato starch.

Pour the batter into the prepared pan and bake for 25 minutes. The cake will seem soft in the middle, cracked, and fallen in on itself—just as if it had been in an earthquake. Covered and held at room temperature, it will keep for 1 week. Serve small slices; it is very rich.

Carlo Middione, the guiding spirit of Vivande, that wonderful Italian restaurant in San Francisco, gave me this recipe and he, in turn, got it from his friend Mirella Nasi from Bologna, Italy. Carlo tells this story about the cake. One of his devoted clients was overheard saying: "You don't think they're going to sell that cake, do you? It looks as if it's been in an earthquake." And thus the name.

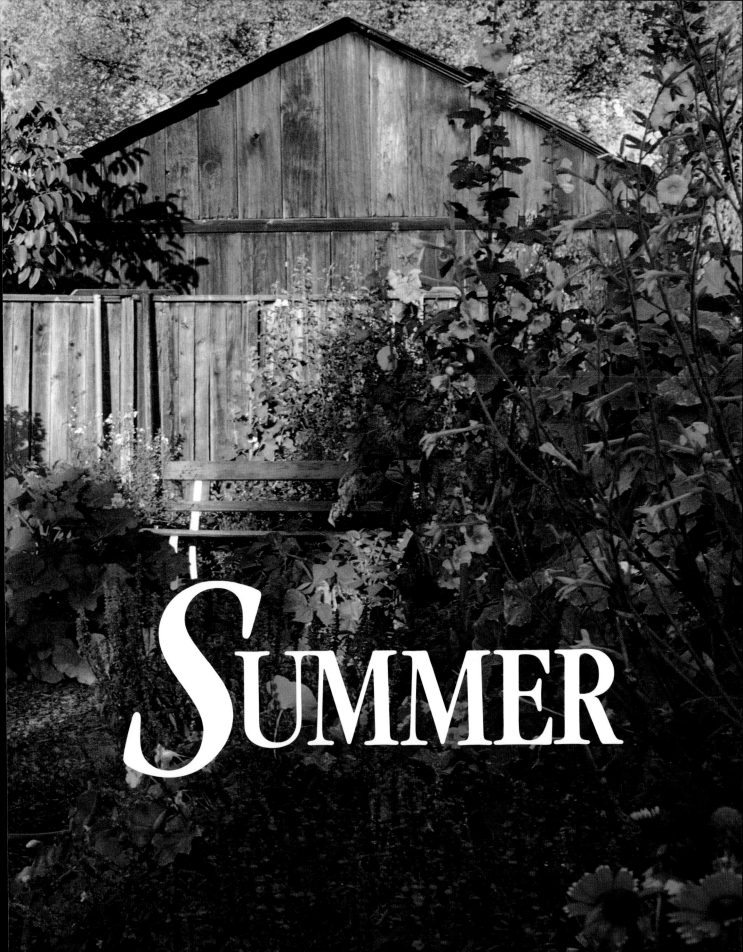

SUMMER

Father's Day

*F*alling in the shadow of graduations, weddings, and that flowery and commercial affair that passes for Mother's Day, Father's Day is a much-overlooked occasion. Why not keep clear of the gift shops and use the day to prepare a dinner with the main man of your family. On Dad's Day, you can safely skip the fish *quenelles* and move on to dishes with more real staying power. Miss Piggy, who clearly knows her way around a satisfying meal, offers Dad one proviso on meals with this kind of allure: "Never eat more than you can lift." The real secret of this dinner is ease—a relaxed convivial feast where all the side dishes can be put together in less than an hour.

ORDER OF PREPARATION

*E*verything here benefits from advance preparation. The grape leaves can be made a day ahead and refrigerated, or let the children stuff and wrap the little packages the day of the dinner. The stuffed leaves should be grilled as friends arrive. Serve them with the grilled French bread. The lamb is best marinated overnight or started the morning of the dinner. Its total cooking time is approximately 30 minutes. The chick-pea and cucumber salads can also be prepared a day ahead.

The steamed pudding takes some time to assemble (20 minutes) and cook (1½ hours) and it must be eaten warm. Start it in the morning or several hours before dinner and reheat it before serving. The cold custard sauce can be done a day ahead. (For light eaters, a serving of some of the fresh blackberries with custard is welcome.)

Wine suggestion: A medium-bodied, complex Pinot Noir will please any dad.

Grape Leaves Stuffed with Goat Cheese, Pine Nuts, and Currants

SERVES 6

5 ounces California goat
  cheese
¼ cup pine nuts
2 tablespoons dried currants

2 tablespoons freshly
  squeezed lemon juice
6 grape leaves, rinsed and
  patted dry
Olive oil

Heat the coals in the grill to medium-hot. With an electric beater or in a food processor, cream the goat cheese until smooth. Set aside.

In a medium-size skillet over medium heat, toast the pine nuts, shaking the pan frequently, until golden brown. Remove from the heat and combine with the goat cheese, currants, and lemon juice. Lay the grape leaves on a flat surface and place 2 tablespoons of the filling in the center of each leaf. Fold into little packages. Brush all over with olive oil and grill on the outer edges of the grill for 1 to 2 minutes. Serve warm with slices of grilled French bread.

Lamb Pinot Noir

SERVES 6

1 5- to 6-pound leg of lamb,
  boned and butterflied (Ask
  your butcher to butterfly
  the lamb for you.)
2 cups fruity virgin olive oil
1 cup Pinot Noir or any dry
  red wine
1 medium-size red onion,
  sliced into thin rounds

3 garlic cloves, peeled and
  thinly sliced
3 large bay leaves
⅓ cup chopped fresh oregano
2 to 3 sprigs fresh rosemary,
  or 3 tablespoons dried
  rosemary
1 teaspoon peppercorns

Put the lamb in a shallow bowl large enough for it to lie flat. Pour the olive oil and Pinot Noir over it. Add the onion, garlic, bay leaves, oregano, rosemary, and peppercorns. Turn once to coat; cover and refrigerate for several hours or overnight, turning the lamb occasionally.

Heat the coals in your grill to medium. Place the lamb on the lowest level of the grill and give it a high fierce heat for 5 minutes on each side; then raise the level of the grill to medium and grill for 8 to 10 minutes on each side or until medium-rare. Transfer to a cutting board and let rest for 10 minutes before cutting on the diagonal into thin slices.

"A man is in general better pleased when he has a good dinner upon the table than when his wife talks Greek."
SAMUEL JOHNSON

*B*utterflied leg of lamb, marinated and grilled, is one of the all-time great summer choices for gatherings of good friends. To impart extraordinary flavor, fuel the fire with bundles of fresh rosemary branches.

STARTING THE FIRE. There is, under the trade name Easy Embers charcoal starter, a tool that provides the surest, simplest, and cheapest method of starting a charcoal fire —and I see no reason why it should not replace the tie as the traditional Father's Day present. With this device, all you need is a couple of sheets of crumpled newspaper to get the coals working—never again will lighter fluid fumes ruin the taste of your perfect marinade. Easy Embers is available at most good hardware stores or from Williams-Sonoma for about $13.

Chick-pea salad, stuffed grape leaves, lamb Pinot Noir—hearty fare for the most important man of the day

Steamed blackberry pudding with cold custard sauce. What Dad wouldn't feel loved?

Greek in inspiration, with a bright confetti appeal.

CHICK-PEA SALAD

SERVES 6

2 19-ounce cans chick-peas, rinsed and drained, or 3 cups dried chick-peas, cooked according to package directions
2 medium-size ripe tomatoes, cored, seeded, and diced
¼ cup chopped sweet green pepper
¼ cup chopped sweet red pepper
4 scallions, trimmed and chopped
¼ cup pitted and halved Greek olives
¼ cup finely chopped fresh Italian parsley
1 tablespoon chopped fresh oregano
½ cup olive oil
3 tablespoons balsamic vinegar
Salt and freshly ground black pepper to taste

In a large serving bowl, combine the chick-peas, tomatoes, green and red peppers, scallions, olives, parsley, and oregano. In a small bowl, whisk together the oil, vinegar, and salt and pepper. Pour the dressing over the salad and toss gently to coat. Let stand at room temperature until ready to serve.

A happy adjunct to any quickly organized summer dinner. Unlike most people, I like my cucumbers crunchy. If you are like me just omit the first step.

CUCUMBER SALAD

SERVES 6

4 cucumbers, peeled and thinly sliced (If you have garden cucumbers, there is no need to peel them.)
2 tablespoons rice vinegar
1 teaspoon coarse salt
½ teaspoon sugar
1 small red onion, peeled and cut into thin rounds
1 cup thinly sliced red radishes
2 to 3 tablespoons chopped fresh dill or fresh mint
Salt and freshly ground black pepper to taste

DRESSING
⅔ cup white wine vinegar
3 tablespoons sugar
2 garlic cloves, peeled and finely chopped
1 tablespoon water
3 tablespoons olive oil

Put the cucumbers in a medium-size bowl and sprinkle on the vinegar, salt, and sugar. Mix well, cover, and let stand for at least 30 minutes.

Drain off all the liquid from the cucumbers; then rinse under cold water and pat them dry. Add the sliced onion, radishes, and dill or mint. Toss gently.

In a small bowl, whisk together the ingredients for the dressing. Pour over the cucumbers and mix well. Season with salt and pepper. Serve at room temperature or slightly chilled.

STEAMED BLACKBERRY PUDDING WITH COLD CUSTARD SAUCE

SERVES 6

½ cup (1 stick) unsalted
    butter
1 cup plus 1 tablespoon
    sugar
2 large eggs, lightly beaten
½ cup honey
    Grated rind of 1 orange
3 cups all-purpose flour
1 teaspoon baking soda
2 teaspoons baking powder

2 teaspoons ground
    cinnamon
¼ cup coarsely chopped
    candied ginger
1 cup buttermilk
2½ cups blackberries
    Cold Custard Sauce
    (recipe follows) or
    whipped cream

In a large bowl, cream the butter and 1 cup of sugar together until light and fluffy. Beat in the eggs, honey, and orange rind.

Sift together the flour, baking soda, baking powder, and cinnamon. Mix in the candied ginger. Add these ingredients to the butter and sugar mixture alternating with the buttermilk. Fold in the blackberries. Thoroughly grease the inside of a 6-cup pudding mold with melted butter. Sprinkle with the 1 tablespoon of sugar and pour in the pudding mixture until the mold is two-thirds full. Cover the mold with aluminum foil and then secure with the lid.

Place the mold on a waterproof trivet in a large kettle. Pour boiling water into the kettle until it comes halfway up the sides of the mold. Cover the kettle with a lid and weight down.

Steam the pudding for 1½ hours, using high heat at first, and then, as the steam builds up, medium-low heat for the rest of the cooking time.

Before unmolding, remove the lid and foil from the mold and allow the pudding to stand for 10 minutes while the excess steam escapes. Unmold onto a serving plate. Serve warm with Cold Custard Sauce or whipped cream. The pudding may be made a day in advance, left in the mold, and reheated for 10 to 15 minutes in boiling water.

COLD CUSTARD SAUCE

MAKES 2 CUPS

4 large egg yolks
½ cup sugar

½ cup Grand Marnier or
    any orange-flavored
    liqueur
½ cup whipping cream

Combine the egg yolks and sugar in the top of a double boiler and beat until pale yellow and thick. Beat in the Grand Marnier and heat the mixture over, not in, simmering water. Beat constantly until very thick. Set the top of the double boiler in a pan of ice and continue to beat until cold.

Whip the cream until stiff and fold into the custard mixture. Cover and refrigerate until ready to serve. This is also delicious over a simple bowl of berries.

In keeping with our nostalgia for American regional foods, steamed puddings are making a comeback. For this recipe you will need the 6-cup steamed pudding mold once common in American kitchens. This generous, blackberry-studded dessert is anything but ordinary summer fare. Make sure to leave room for it. It will fill you to the brim.

INVEST IN A SET OF HORSESHOES. Men take to this game. Fathers and sons take to it. The metallic thud of the horseshoes hitting the pole is pure nostalgia. An old saying goes: "*Almost* counts only with horseshoes."

Intensity and balance—grilled tuna with wasabi butter, and cummerbund potatoes

A Beauteous Evening

*T*he summer solstice—sometimes falling on June 21, sometimes on June 22—signals the arrival of true summer and affords us something else very much worth celebrating: the longest day of the year. On this day the sun sets very late, twilight lingers, flowers glow pale and starry in the garden, and the only event is to watch the shadows lengthen on the grass as the daylight disappears. Of all nights of the year, choose this one to serve a leisurely and romantic dinner for friends out of doors. Invite the people you most enjoy and sit long, long at the table, talking on into the evening as summer makes its entrance, for, as M.F.K. Fisher said, "...friends should have the rare gift of sitting. They should be able, no—eager to sit for hours—three, four, six—over a meal of soup and wine and cheese, as well as one of twenty fabulous courses."

I have composed a menu of soft colors to reflect the tranquil mood of the evening. The minted potatoes and cucumbers will cool the palate. Even the fish, when raw, is of a delicate pastel pink and, once cooked, is dressed at serving time with the pistachio-tinted wasabi butter. Highly seasonal right now is the radish, that traditional "first" from the vegetable garden. I have chosen a dessert of cherries for this moment because the presence of cherries in the stores at this time of year always tells me "summer is here."

M·e·n·u

RADISHES
WITH COARSE SALT

·

BABY BEETS
WITH BEET GREENS

·

GRILLED TUNA
WITH WASABI BUTTER

·

CUMMERBUND POTATOES
WITH CUCUMBERS AND MINT

·

CHERRY ROLY-POLY
WITH CHERRY SAUCE

Luscious radishes ready for salt

ORDER OF PREPARATION

*T*he cherry roly-poly can be made, with its sauce, a day ahead or early in the morning of the day of the dinner. It should be reheated and served piping hot. Marinate the tuna steaks for at least 30 minutes before grilling them. You will need about 15 minutes to prepare the beets and 40 minutes for baking them; set the chopped greens aside until the last minute. Chop the cucumbers and set them aside. Start the fire for the grilling. Next, start pan-roasting the potatoes. Make the wasabi butter. Add the cucumbers to the potatoes. Prepare the beet greens. Now grill the tuna steaks at the last moment, and top each portion with a teaspoon or more (for those who like theirs hot) of wasabi butter.

Wine suggestion: Offer a rich, fruity Pinot Noir.

RADISHES WITH COARSE SALT

SERVES 6

*R*adishes are most plentiful from May to July and provide lovely color and a crisp texture. When buying radishes, look for well-formed, plump firm radishes with fresh green tops.

Wash 2 bunches medium-size red radishes thoroughly, cut off the tops and rootlets. Serve ice cold with coarse Kosher salt.

BABY BEETS WITH BEET GREENS

SERVES 6

*S*weet-tasting with a lovely deep hue, these are the most tender beets imaginable. Once you've cooked beets in this manner, you will never boil them again. Look for "Little Ball" (a true "baby" beet) or Golden beets.

16 to 20 baby beets, ½- to
    1-inch diameter
3 tablespoons coarsely
    chopped shallots
6 tablespoons unsalted
    butter

3 tablespoons olive oil
Salt and freshly ground
    black pepper to taste
Juice of 1 orange
Grated rind of 1 orange

Preheat the oven to 375° F.

Wash the beets in warm water. Cut the stems off approximately 1 inch above the top of the beets and reserve the green tops. Put the beets on a baking sheet. Bake small beets for 20 to 30 minutes and large beets for 1 hour or until just fork-tender. Peel under cool running water; then drain.

Meanwhile, coarsely chop the beet greens, leaving whole any small tender leaves.

In a large skillet, sauté the shallots in 2 tablespoons of the butter until limp and lightly colored. Add the oil and 2 more tablespoons of the butter along with the beet greens. Cook, partially covered, until just wilted. Season with salt and pepper.

Melt the remaining 2 tablespoons of butter in a saucepan. Add the orange juice, grated orange rind, and beets. Cook, stirring, over low heat until the beets are warmed through. Serve the beets on a bed of the wilted beet greens.

GRILLED TUNA WITH WASABI BUTTER

SERVES 6

6 5-ounce tuna steaks
¼ cup olive oil
   Juice of 1 lemon
2 tablespoons peeled fresh
   ginger, pressed through a
   garlic press

6 tablespoons unsalted
   butter, softened
¼ cup wasabi (powdered
   horseradish)
   Salt and freshly ground
   black pepper

Heat the coals to medium-hot.

Lay the tuna steaks in a large shallow pan in one layer. Combine the olive oil, lemon juice, and ginger in a small bowl and pour over the fish. Let sit for 20 to 30 minutes while you prepare the rest of the dinner. Turn the fish once in the marinade. Mix the butter and wasabi together into a thick paste. Set aside.

Season the steaks lightly with salt and pepper and grill them for about 7 to 10 minutes, turning them over two or three times. Tuna dries out quickly so keep it moist with the marinade while cooking. Transfer the steaks to a platter and top each one with a teaspoon or tablespoon of the wasabi butter. Serve at once.

*T*his dish is a Western adaptation of Japanese sushi for those who don't like their fish raw. A butter of wasabi is a variant of the thick green paste of horseradish and mustard powder mixed with water that traditionally accompanies sushi. Here I have mixed the wasabi powder with softened butter and melted it over grilled, rather than raw, tuna.

Tuna has escaped the confines of the can and is now readily available in its fresh form at many fish markets. When it is grilled, fresh tuna is a fish that has found its moment.

CUMMERBUND POTATOES WITH CUCUMBERS AND MINT

SERVES 6

3 pounds red new potatoes
⅓ cup unsalted butter
6 garlic cloves, peeled and
   finely minced
⅓ cup water
1 tablespoon coarse salt, or
   to taste
1 large bunch fresh mint
   with stems removed, finely
   chopped

2 large cucumbers, peeled,
   seeded, and cut into
   ½-inch cubes
   Freshly ground black
   pepper to taste
GARNISH
   Chopped chives

Using a carrot peeler, remove a spiral of skin from each potato. Choose a deep skillet large enough to hold all the vegetables in more or less one layer. Melt the butter and sauté the garlic over medium heat for 1 to 2 minutes. Do not let it brown. Add the potatoes, water, salt, and mint. Cover and cook over medium-low heat for 15 to 20 minutes, shaking the pan occasionally to rotate the potatoes, so they all get brown. Add the cucumbers and cook for 10 minutes more or until the cucumbers begin to wilt. Season generously with pepper and additional salt, if necessary, and garnish with the chives.

*M*y favorite way to "roast" potatoes without having to heat up the oven. The sautéed cucumbers and mint refresh the palate after the fiery wasabi butter.

CHERRY ROLY-POLY WITH CHERRY SAUCE

SERVES 6

3 cups pastry flour	1 tablespoon all-purpose flour
¾ teaspoon salt	3 tablespoons unsalted butter
2 tablespoons baking powder	
1½ tablespoons cold unsalted butter	GLAZE
1½ cups heavy cream	1 large egg yolk, beaten
2 pounds fresh cherries pitted, or 2 17-ounce cans cherries in light syrup or juice, drained	1 tablespoon heavy cream
	Cherry Sauce (recipe follows)
2 to 3 tablespoons sugar	1 cup whipping cream, beaten until very stiff

Preheat the oven to 350° F.

In a bowl, sift together the flour, salt, and baking powder; add the cold butter and rub it in with your fingertips. Add the cream; mix to a soft dough. Turn out onto a lightly floured board; knead for 3 to 5 minutes or until smooth. Pat and roll to a rectangle approximately 10 × 12 inches, 1 to 2 inches thick. Reserve a 2-inch piece for cutting out decorations. Place the pastry rectangle on a buttered baking sheet.

Distribute the cherries over the dough and sprinkle with the sugar and flour; dot with the butter. Roll up like a jelly roll; then moisten and press the overlapping edge and close the ends as securely as possible. Cut 9 to 10 ½-inch rounds from the reserved dough to represent cherries and 3 thin strips for stems. Moisten one side with water and decorate the top with cut-out cherry designs. Brush the dough all over with the glaze and bake for 25 minutes. Serve surrounded by the Cherry Sauce and whipped cream.

CHERRY SAUCE

MAKES 3 CUPS

1 cup Amaretto liqueur	2 cups fresh or canned pitted cherries, drained of their juices
½ cup sugar	
½ cup red currant jelly	
Juice of 1 lemon	

Mix all the ingredients together in a saucepan except the cherries, and cook over low heat until reduced to a syrup. Add the cherries and heat through. Serve hot.

A ladylike cherry roly-poly

Far Niente

*A*ugust. The "dog days." It's hot outside, it's hot inside—and no one feels like cooking. More to the point, no one wants to slave in a hot kitchen or over a fiery grill. This *far niente* ("without care") dinner, perfect for a warm summer night, is one of the easiest I know how to prepare. The menu is perfect because the recipes require little cooking and almost everything is served at room temperature.

The dinner is Italian from top to bottom. Now, in Italian cooking there is no such thing as just a little garlic. This menu features it. Don't stint. You are all in this together.

ORDER OF PREPARATION

*S*tart by making the tomato sauce, cover and set it aside for at least an hour. Beat the ricotta until smooth, and refrigerate. Arrange the antipasto. It can happily sit out at room temperature. Wash and dry the greens and put them in a salad bowl, cover, and refrigerate. As your friends arrive make the bruschetta. Toast plenty: People tend to eat this as fast as you can make it. Spirit away what you can, cover, and keep warm in a low oven until dinner. Have your friends help themselves to Campari and antipasto while you start the water boiling for the pasta. Put the pasta in to cook and —this is important—urge your guests to *sit down* at the table: Once the pasta is cooked it must be served immediately. Toss the salad with the oil and vinegar. Drain the pasta and toss with some of the sauce, arrange on warm plates with more sauce, and serve at once. You can assemble the dessert while you make the espresso.

Wine suggestion: If you prefer wine over Campari, substitute a fine Italian Cabernet Sauvignon.

CAMPARI AND SODA

The classic version calls for 2 ounces of Campari poured over ice and then mixed with club soda, with an added twist of lemon or lime. Freshly squeezed orange juice, ginger ale, or tonic water can be substituted for the soda if you wish.

*H*ot and humid summer days make us yearn for some cool, refreshing liquid. Campari with soda has a pale pink color and a slightly bitter taste. It is one of my favorite summer drinks.

ANTIPASTO

CHOOSE FROM THE FOLLOWING:

Peperoncini
Red and yellow peppers
in wine vinegar
Anchovies
Marinated artichoke
hearts
Assorted olives

Assorted pickled
vegetables
Prosciutto or bresaola
with melon
Fresh or smoked
mozzarella

*A*ntipasto is one of the best-loved features of an Italian meal. With a well-stocked pantry, the preparation is quick and direct. An antipasto can be incredibly varied, but for dinner at home, tarry over a few select items. Remember that this is meant to tease the appetite, not satisfy it. A little of what you like is best.

MUSHROOMS COOKED IN GRAPE LEAVES

SERVES 6

12 fresh or bottled grape
leaves
3/4 cup virgin olive oil
1/2 cup white wine vinegar
36 (about 3 pounds)
medium-size mushrooms,
wiped clean and trimmed

1 lemon, cut into thin slices
and seeded
2 garlic cloves, peeled but
left whole
1 bay leaf
2 to 3 thyme sprigs
1/4 teaspoon whole black
peppercorns

*T*his is one of my favorite recipes and makes a delicious addition to the antipasto. It is adapted from a recipe included in Elizabeth David's *Summer Cooking*.

Preheat the oven to 300° F.

If you are using fresh grape leaves, blanch them in salted boiling water for 3 minutes; then drain and pat them dry. Or, under cold running water, rinse the brine from the appropriate number of canned leaves and pat them dry.

Arrange half the leaves in the bottom of a nonaluminum casserole with lid. Pour one third of the olive oil and one third of the vinegar over them and layer the mushrooms on top. Tuck in the lemon slices, garlic, bay leaf, thyme sprigs, and peppercorns. Pour a little more olive oil and vinegar on top, cover with the remaining leaves, olive oil, and vinegar.

Cover the casserole and bring to a simmer on the top of the stove. Transfer to the oven and bake for 30 to 35 minutes. Remove and discard the top layer of grape leaves before serving.

This is one of the easiest and most delicious of all pasta dishes. There are many variations around of this classic but you should really only attempt them in the summer when tomatoes are at their ripest, plucked fresh from the vine, still warm from the sun. The golden jubilee tomatoes give the sauce a bright splash of color. Never available in a supermarket, they are sometimes to be found at well-stocked greengrocers. Grow them in your garden; they are as easy to grow as standard tomatoes.

FRESH UNCOOKED TOMATO SAUCE WITH THREE PASTAS

SERVES 6

4 to 5 cups cored and
  finely chopped red and
  yellow ripe tomatoes
3 garlic cloves, peeled and
  finely minced
¼ cup minced fresh basil
2 tablespoons minced fresh
  oregano
2 teaspoons salt
7 tablespoons virgin olive
  oil

½ pound Taleggio or
  Fontina cheese, cut into
  1-inch cubes
Juice of 1 lemon
Freshly ground black
  pepper to taste
1½ to 2 pounds of a
  combination of penne
  (tubes), fusilli (spirals),
  and conchiglie (shells)

GARNISH
Freshly chopped basil

In a bowl, combine the chopped tomatoes and their juice with the garlic, basil, oregano, salt, and 6 tablespoons of the olive oil. Mix well. Add the cheese, cover, and marinate at room temperature for at least 1 hour. Just before serving add the lemon juice and freshly ground pepper.

Cook the pasta according to the package directions. Drain and return to the cooking pot. Add the remaining tablespoon of olive oil and season with salt and pepper.

Pour half the sauce on the cooked pasta and toss.

Because the pasta cools very quickly, this dish is best portioned onto warm individual serving plates. Serve the remaining sauce on top of each portion. Garnish with a little chopped basil if you wish. Pass the garlic toast.

BRUSCHETTA

SERVES 6

12 1½-inch slices Italian
  bread (preferably whole
  wheat)

4 to 6 garlic cloves, split
  open and smashed
¼ cup fruity virgin olive oil
  Coarse salt

Preheat the broiler.

Toast the bread on both sides under the broiler until lightly brown. While the bread is still warm, rub one side with a smashed garlic clove. Use new cloves as you move along. Brush each slice generously with olive oil and sprinkle with coarse salt. Keep warm until ready to serve.

The toasting of this Italian garlic bread is a good task for a guest who doesn't mind having his hands smell of garlic.

ABOVE: Fresh uncooked tomato sauce made with red and yellow tomatoes—a cool dish for a hot summer night

BELOW: A sensuous dolce of creamy pale ricotta, ripe peaches, raspberries, and honey

*F*ragrant ripe peaches and creamy pale ricotta enhanced by the flavor of local honey—the essence of Tuscan summer is in these things and I offer this dessert to you with a *bravissima* (I choose the feminine ending because the dessert has definite female qualities).

ITALIAN FIREFLIES. The firefly is not as much with us as it used to be. Something in our environment is cutting down its glimmering population. Here is a game with a man-made substitute that has something of the ghostly magic of the original.

While still at the table, take the leftover wrapping papers of the Amaretti cookies and roll lengthwise into a tight roll as if you were rolling a cigarette. Stand a paper vertically on a flat surface (any wind makes this impossible). Light the top edge and wait for the flame to burn down the length of the paper. At the final moment of burning, the paper will magically lift off into the night sky. The highest flying paper wins. More dessert! (The secret of success lies in how tightly you roll the paper.)

INSALATA MISTA

SERVES 6

4 to 5 cups fresh greens, such as arugula, endive, curly chicory or escarole, or Bibb, red leaf, or Boston lettuces
Coarse salt to taste

2 to 3 tablespoons olive oil
½ to 1 tablespoon balsamic vinegar
Freshly ground black pepper to taste

Rinse and dry the lettuce. Tear the larger leaves into small pieces. Sprinkle with coarse salt and add a tablespoon of oil at a time to just coat the leaves. Add the vinegar and toss gently but well. Serve immediately. Pass the pepper mill at the table.

DOLCE OF RICOTTA, PEACHES, AND HONEY

SERVES 6

2 cups fresh whole-milk ricotta cheese

5 to 6 large ripe peaches
Honey to taste

In a mixing bowl, beat the ricotta until smooth. Pile it in the center of a large serving plate. Slice the peaches and place them around the ricotta. Dribble the honey all over. (If they are available, toss in a few raspberries for added color.) Serve at room temperature with store-bought Amaretti cookies and espresso.

No-Catch-of-the-Day Al Fresco

M·e·n·u

DEVILED EGGS
·
ASSORTED
RAW VEGETABLES
·
TOMATO SANDWICHES
·
PAIN BAGNAT
·
PLUMS AND
CHAMPAGNE GRAPES
·
MEXICAN CORN CAKE
·
ICED CAFÉ AU LAIT
·
BEER
·
WINE

*T*he great French gastronome Brillat-Savarin understood the charms of the informal picnic, and of some happy picnickers he wrote: "Seating themselves on the green sward they eat while the corks fly and there is talk, laughter and merriment, and perfect freedom, for the universe is their drawing room and the sun their lamp. Besides, they have appetite, nature's special gift, which lends to such a meal a vivacity unknown indoors, however beautiful the surroundings." When the urge for dining in the open comes over you, be both adventurous and carefree. Carry your picnic late in the day beyond the lighted patio to a special rustic hideaway, eschew the caravan of hampers packed with fine nappery and fragile glasses, and take only what's necessary; throw a traditional red-checked tablecloth over the grass and enjoy this easily transportable but gracious meal. If you must pretend to have a reason for a picnic, take fishing rod and tackle with you to a lake- or stream-side setting, and when your party catches nothing at all, fuel up the fire for the pain bagnat and rest assured that the food you have brought will more than satisfy your guests. The trick is to travel light to the picnic site, use basic traditional equipment once settled in there, stretch out on the ground, and let nature and the rising moon take care of the rest.

ORDER OF PREPARATION

*S*tart the cooking the night before the event by preparing the corn cake. It benefits from sitting overnight. Leave it in the pan and cover with aluminum foil. It is much less apt to break in transit that way.

The morning of the picnic you can make the eggs, rinse the fruit, and wash and cut the vegetables, keeping them crisp in ice water in the refrigerator until you are ready to leave. Make the pain bagnat either the night before or the day of the picnic, allowing 40 minutes for assembly. The loaves need to sit weighted down for an hour. The tomato sandwiches can be thrown together at the last minute. To pack for the picnic, simply wrap the various dishes in newspaper (a handy natural insulator), tie the packages with some red cord, place everything in any basket or makeshift hamper, and head for the hills.

Wine suggestions: Picnic with a fruity Chardonnay or even a zesty Zinfandel. If you prefer beer, select something light and tart.

Pain bagnat on the grill

*Tomato sandwiches and deviled eggs—
American classics*

For me, no picnic is complete without deviled eggs. You can get fancy with all types of fillings, adding anything from anchovy paste to chopped salami and olives. I prefer the old-fashioned plain filling, but have reluctantly taken to adding a pinch of fresh herbs for those of you who can't leave well enough alone.

DEVILED EGGS
SERVES 6

6 extra-large fresh eggs
2 tablespoons unsalted butter, softened
1 tablespoon Dijon mustard
1/3 cup mayonnaise, preferably homemade

1 tablespoon mixed, finely minced fresh herbs, such as chervil, parsley, or tarragon (If you don't have access to fresh herbs, eliminate this ingredient.)

Put the eggs in a saucepan large enough to hold them in one layer and add cold water to cover. Bring to a simmer and cook for 12 to 15 minutes, counting from the time the water begins to simmer.

Drain the eggs and immediately plunge them into cold water while you crack and peel them.

Halve the eggs lengthwise. Press the yolks through a sieve and combine with the butter, mustard, mayonnaise, and half the fresh herbs. With a pastry bag fitted with a large decorative tip or with a tablespoon, stuff each egg white half with an equal portion of the filling. Press the halves together gently. Garnish the eggs with the remaining chopped herbs.

Place each egg in the center of a square of wax paper and twist the ends. Keep refrigerated until ready to transport. Serve at room temperature.

Once summer's tomatoes have ripened on the vine, these sandwiches should be eaten all season long, at every occasion, at every meal. Have them while you can: Some things are just too good to let go by.

TOMATO SANDWICHES
SERVES 6

1 cup mayonnaise, preferably homemade
12 slices firm white sandwich bread
2 medium-size red onions, cut into paper-thin slices

1 cup fresh basil, washed and patted dry
3 to 4 vine-ripened red tomatoes, sliced
Salt and freshly ground black pepper to taste

Spread equal amounts of the mayonnaise on one side of each slice of bread. Arrange 2 rounds of onion on half the slices. Cover the onion with several basil leaves and slices of tomato. Season the tomatoes generously with salt and pepper. Top with 2 more rounds of onion and the remaining slices of bread. Cut on the diagonal. Wrap in wax paper or plastic wrap. Do not refrigerate.

INCLUDE IN YOUR PICNIC HAMPER OR CRATE this individual package for each guest: a large clear plastic storage bag packed with 2 cups, plastic knife and fork, 2 to 3 napkins, and 2 paper plates. Wrap the knife and fork in the napkins, roll and place inside the cups. Tie with a twist. The bag can double as a garbage bag, and all your "breakables" can be left at home.

PAIN BAGNAT

SERVES 6

1 long loaf Italian or French
bread, halved lengthwise
1 cup pitted and chopped
Niçoise, Greek, or Italian
olives
1 9-ounce jar roasted red
and yellow peppers,
drained, patted dry, and
chopped
4 to 6 scallions, minced
1 6-ounce jar marinated
artichoke hearts, sliced
2 large eggs, hard-boiled,
chopped

8 to 12 ounces cold roasted
chicken, thinly sliced or
poached (see Note)
1 bunch fresh watercress
with stems removed
8 to 12 ounces Provolone,
thinly sliced

DRESSING
1 large bunch fresh parsley
½ bunch fresh watercress
1 garlic clove, smashed
4 anchovy fillets, rinsed and
patted dry
2 tablespoons drained capers
Juice of 1 lemon
½ cup olive oil

Scoop out the soft inside from both sides of the loaf, leaving an approximately
½-inch-thick shell.

In a bowl, combine the olives, peppers, scallions, artichoke hearts, and chopped
eggs.

Make the dressing: In a food processor or blender, purée the parsley, watercress,
garlic, anchovies, capers, and lemon juice. Add the oil in a thin stream and blend
until the dressing is thick.

Add ¼ cup of the dressing to the olive mixture to bind it. Spread the remaining
dressing generously on the hollow bread shells.

Arrange on one half of the loaf some of the watercress and a few slices of cheese
and chicken. Mound half of the olive mixture in the shell, packing gently but firmly.
Repeat with the other half.

Put the two halves firmly together and seal tightly in aluminum foil or plastic
wrap. Place a cutting board or baking sheet on top of the sandwich; then place a
5-pound weight on top of the board or sheet. Refrigerate for *at least* 30 minutes or
until ready to transport. (This may be made the night before.)

To grill, brush the inside of a hand-held basket-type grill with olive oil. Cut the
sandwich in half and place the halves inside the grill; close the grill. Toast over
medium coals, turning frequently until the bread is lightly browned and the cheese
melts. Cut into 2-inch wedges with a serrated knife. Serve immediately.

NOTE: A quick way to prepare the chicken is to simmer one cutlet for 12 to 15
minutes in 1 cup of chicken broth to which 1 bay leaf, 1 celery top, and 1 sprig of
thyme or tarragon have been added.

A happy marriage of all the best ingredients
from the Provençal coast of the Mediterra-
nean. This overstuffed loaf sandwich is a meal
in itself.

D isasters

can accompany picnics. In fact, a simple

omission of one essential piece of

equipment can mean *certain* disaster. Some

take-alongs to ward off catastrophe:

flashlight

matches

Swiss army knife

garbage bag

corkscrew

and

bug spray

bug spray

bug spray

A Mexican corn cake with fruit—perfect picnic food

MEXICAN CORN CAKE

SERVES 6

1 cup all-purpose flour
1 cup yellow cornmeal
1 cup granulated sugar
½ cup blanched almonds,
   toasted for 3 to 4 minutes
   and finely ground
Grated rind of 1 lemon

2 large egg yolks, lightly
   beaten
Juice of 1 lemon
½ cup (1 stick) unsalted
   butter, softened
2 tablespoons confectioners'
   sugar

Butter an 8-inch springform pan. Preheat the oven to 350° F.

In a large bowl, combine the flour, cornmeal, granulated sugar, ground almonds, and lemon rind. Add the egg yolks and lemon juice to the dry ingredients, mixing with your fingers until the texture resembles oatmeal. Work in the softened butter as if you were making a piecrust. (This works very well in a food processor.) Gather the dough into a ball and lightly press into the springform pan. Sprinkle the confectioners' sugar over the top and bake for 35 to 40 minutes or until a skewer inserted near the center comes out clean. Serve at room temperature, cut into wedges.

"**O**h!
You who have been a-fishing
will endorse me when I say,
That it always is the biggest fish
you catch that gets away."
EUGENE FIELD

Independence Day

Cookies and ice cream; cool toppings for a crackling celebration

*E*ven in America we are comforted by tradition. Almost every holiday, whether it be European or American in origin, religious or secular in nature, has foods that are associated with it. Turkey at Thanksgiving and fruit cake at Christmas are some obvious examples. On the Fourth of July, our thoughts turn to classic American fare—hamburgers, corn, tomatoes, ice cream. This menu, a family meal with plenty of food that children like, is a collection of updated backyard favorites. Have fun with it—this is a celebration. Go all out with paper decorations, wave the flag, get some competitive games going on the lawn, set off firecrackers (well *away* from children). Use all your red, white, and blue dishes and try to inveigle your guests into coming dressed in the same colors. Sure it's corny, but I've been a party to a red, white, and blue-garbed Fourth and the comical effect of a tri-colored crowd added considerable enthusiasm to the proceedings. July marks the beginning of berry season. Make sure to have a big dish of strawberries and blueberries at dessert time for those revelers who want to steer clear of the sumptuous cookies and cream.

You will be able to join in the fun. Nothing on this menu is cooked inside unless, lacking space on the grill, you opt to cook the corn on top of the stove.

M·e·n·u

POCKET BURGERS

·

POTATO CRISPS

·

FIRECRACKER TOMATO SALAD

·

CORN ON THE COB
WITH FLAVORED BUTTER

·

GRILLED RED ONIONS
WITH MINT

·

COOKIES AND CREAM

·

STRAWBERRIES
AND BLUEBERRIES

Order of Preparation

*I*t is worth noting that the preparation of the stuffings and butters takes some time, although they can all be made a day ahead and refrigerated. The butters should be brought to room temperature before they are smeared on the corn. I bake the potatoes the night before as well; then wrap and store in the refrigerator overnight. Scoop out the pulp just before grilling. The cookies and cream should be made a day ahead and frozen solid.

While the coals are heating up, wrap the onions in aluminum foil and cut up the tomato salad. Bury the onions in the coals 30 to 40 minutes before you are ready to eat them. Have all the fillings handy and set out the hamburgers for friends to stuff to their liking. Grill the corn while the burgers cook.

Make a big display of condiments and add-ons: butter, mustard, catsup, mayonnaise; lettuce, spinach, or wilted Swiss chard; buns and rolls.

Serve the fruit and cookies and cream during the fireworks.

Wine suggestion: Celebrate with a medium-bodied, zesty Zinfandel.

Pocket Burgers

SERVES 6

A new twist on an old favorite. Pocket burgers ooze from the inside where they hide a delicious surprise. You can be creative with the stuffings or leave well enough alone. For a special topping, try wilted Swiss chard leaves or spinach instead of lettuce. Note to the chef: Burgers are serious business and all good cooks still treat them with reverence.

4 pounds ground lean chuck or top round

Salt and freshly ground black pepper to taste

Season the meat with salt and pepper and divide it into 6 to 8 large oval and fairly thick patties. Make a hole or pocket in the center of each patty; fill with 1½ to 2 tablespoons of one of the fillings (see recipes below) or have guests do this for themselves later at the grill. Cover the filling with more meat. Grill over moderate coals for 8 minutes on each side for medium-rare burgers. Serve with hard rolls or sourdough rolls from a good bakery.

Marvelous Mexican Filling

¼ cup vegetable oil
3 green chiles, chopped
2 medium-size onions, finely chopped
6 garlic cloves, peeled and minced

¼ cup chopped fresh coriander
6 ounces Monterey Jack cheese, shredded
Salt and freshly ground black pepper to taste

In a large skillet, heat the oil over medium heat. Add the chiles, onions, and garlic and sauté until the onions are translucent and soft. Cool completely before sprinkling the coriander and grated cheese over the mixture. Season with salt and pepper and blend well.

ITALIAN FILLING

¾ pound Gorgonzola cheese,
    crumbled
½ cup (1 stick) unsalted
    butter, softened

4 tablespoons minced fresh
    basil

In a bowl, mash the Gorgonzola cheese and butter into a paste. Add the minced basil and blend well.

TAPENADE FILLING

½ cup pitted purple olives
    (see Note)
¼ cup pitted green olives
3 anchovy fillets
1 garlic clove, peeled and
    minced
2 tablespoons drained capers

1 tablespoon freshly
    squeezed lemon juice
1 cup chopped fresh parsley
¼ cup virgin olive oil
    Freshly ground black
    pepper to taste

In a blender or food processor, combine the olives, anchovy fillets, garlic, capers, lemon juice, and parsley. Process until smooth. With the motor running, add the olive oil, a little at a time, as if making mayonnaise, to make a thick sauce. Add a few grindings of pepper. (The tapenade will keep refrigerated for up to 1 week.)

NOTE: For best flavor, buy olives with pits and remove pits with a small, sharp knife or cherry pitter.

POTATO CRISPS

SERVES 6

6 extra-large russet potatoes,
    scrubbed and dried
One of the flavored butters
    (page 92) (I like the chile-
    cumin butter best here.)

GARNISH
    Chopped fresh coriander
    Coarse salt
    Freshly ground black pepper to
    taste

Preheat the oven to 425° F.

Pierce the potatoes in several places to allow steam to escape during baking. Bake for 1 hour or until tender. Cool completely.

Cut the potatoes lengthwise into four wedges. Gently scoop out most of the potato pulp, leaving a thin layer all around. Reserve the pulp for another use (see Note).

Use a pastry brush to lightly coat the inside of the potato wedges with softened flavored butter. Grill briefly over moderate coals, skin-side up, until hot and charred.

Have dishes of chopped coriander, coarse salt, and freshly ground pepper nearby for garnish.

NOTE: The potato pulp may be used the next day for potato pancakes or combined with lots of butter and sharp cheese and baked in the oven.

LAWN GAMES, AMERICAN-STYLE: To stimulate the appetite, a good game of croquet works wonders. For the Fourth, it must be the American version of the sport—hard-hitting, somewhat imprecise, impolite. A highly competitive game of kickball will fulfill the same function. Remember: All's fair in love and war.

*T*he potatoes should be baked the night before or on the morning of the dinner and the skins grilled at the last minute.

Colorful firecracker tomato salad made from perfectly ripe beefsteak, Italian Roma, and golden jubilee tomatoes

FIRECRACKER TOMATO SALAD

SERVES 6

3 beefsteak tomatoes, cut into thick slices
5 Italian Roma tomatoes, cut in half
3 golden jubilee tomatoes, cut into wedges

½ cup small fresh basil leaves
Sea salt and freshly ground black pepper to taste
Virgin olive oil (optional)

Toss the tomatoes with the basil leaves and sprinkle with salt and pepper. Serve plain or with a few dribbles of oil.

NOTE: Other varieties of tomatoes you can use are Golden Round, Tiger Striped, Red Cherry, and Yellow Pear.

CORN ON THE COB WITH FLAVORED BUTTER

SERVES 6

Corn on the cob dressed with three different compound butters

12 ears freshly picked sweet
   corn

½ cup (1 stick) unsalted
   butter, softened (or one of
   the flavored butters on
   page 92)

Gently peel back the corn husks, but leave them attached at the base. Remove all corn silk. (This step can be very tedious; see if you can talk some older children into helping.) Rub the soft butter all over the corn kernels. Fold the husks back over the corn and tie them in place with kitchen twine or a strip of one of the corn husks. Grill over moderate coals for 8 to 10 minutes, turning them frequently, until the outer leaves are lightly charred.

CORN VARIETIES. You cannot go wrong with any of these—Iochief Hybrid (sweet, all yellow), Butter and Sugar (mixed yellow and white kernels with a high sugar content, delicious), and the pearly late-season Silver Queen (all white).

RED PEPPER BUTTER

MAKES ABOUT ½ CUP

2 medium-size red peppers,
  or 1 7-ounce jar roasted
  peppers, drained and
  patted dry

½ cup (1 stick) unsalted
  butter, softened
Pinch of cayenne pepper
½ teaspoon dried thyme

Char the peppers on all sides over an open flame or under the broiler, turning every 5 minutes or until the skin is blackened all over. Put the peppers in a plastic or brown paper bag and let them steam until cool. Remove the peppers from the bag and peel off the charred skin. Cut off the top and discard seeds and ribs.

In a food processor or blender, purée the roasted pepper; then add the butter a little at a time, blending well after each addition. Add the cayenne and thyme and blend the mixture well. Transfer to a bowl, cover, and refrigerate until ready to use. (This butter may be made up to 3 days in advance.) Serve at room temperature.

BASIL BUTTER

MAKES ABOUT ½ CUP

1 cup loosely packed fresh
  basil leaves

½ cup (1 stick) unsalted
  butter, softened

In a food processor, mince the basil leaves; then add the butter a little at a time until well blended. Transfer to a bowl, cover, and refrigerate until ready to use. (The basil butter may be made up to 3 days in advance.) Serve at room temperature.

CHILE-CUMIN BUTTER

MAKES ABOUT ½ CUP

2 teaspoons ground Ancho
  chile, roasted and peeled,
  or 2 canned jalapeños,
  finely chopped

½ teaspoon ground cumin
½ cup (1 stick) unsalted
  butter, softened

Beat the chile and cumin into the softened butter in a bowl. Cover and refrigerate until ready to use. Serve at room temperature.

*M*ake this at least one day in advance for the deepest flavor.

GRILLED RED ONIONS WITH MINT

SERVES 6

3 to 4 medium-size
  unpeeled red onions, cut
  in half
1 cup chopped fresh mint
¼ cup chopped fresh oregano
Salt

Sugar
6 to 8 teaspoons unsalted
  butter
Red wine vinegar
Freshly ground black
  pepper to taste

Place 2 halves of an onion on a square of heavy-duty aluminum foil. Sprinkle with a little chopped mint, oregano, a pinch each of salt and sugar, and ½ teaspoon of butter. Twist the ends to seal. Repeat for all onions. Bury the foil-wrapped onions in the glowing coals and cook for 30 to 45 minutes, turning several times. Remove from the foil and arrange on a platter. Before serving sprinkle with vinegar and freshly ground pepper.

COOKIES AND CREAM

SERVES 6

3 pints ice cream in assorted flavors (see Note)　　*24 Chocolate Wafers (recipe follows)*

To assemble the sandwiches, soften the ice cream at room temperature for approximately 15 minutes. Peel away the cardboard containers and cut the ice cream into ½-inch-thick rounds. Put 1 round between 2 cookies and press together gently. Put the sandwiches on a platter or tray, cover tightly with aluminum foil or plastic wrap, and freeze until serving time. These sandwiches may be made several days in advance, but they must be kept well-covered in the freezer. Serve frozen.

NOTE: Try filling the sandwiches with orange cream, pistachio, strawberry, or French vanilla ice cream or raspberry sherbet.

The sandwiches can also be made with your favorite chocolate chip or oatmeal cookie.

CHOCOLATE WAFERS

MAKES TWENTY-FOUR 3-INCH ROUNDS

1 cup all-purpose flour
½ teaspoon baking soda
½ teaspoon salt
4 ounces semisweet chocolate chips
6 ounces unsweetened chocolate

¼ cup (½ stick) unsalted butter, softened
½ cup granulated sugar
½ cup firmly packed dark brown sugar
1 large egg
1½ teaspoons vanilla extract

Sift together the flour, baking soda, and salt. Set aside. Melt the chocolates with the butter in the top of a double boiler, covered, over hot water. Remove from the heat, stir in the sugars, egg, and vanilla until smooth and shiny.

Transfer the chocolate mixture to a large bowl and gradually add the sifted ingredients, stirring just to blend. Chill the dough in the refrigerator for about 15 minutes.

Preheat the oven to 375° F. Roll the cookie dough out on a lightly floured surface to a thickness of ¼ inch. Use a 3-inch fluted cookie cutter to cut the cookies from the dough. Place 1 inch apart on an ungreased baking sheet. Bake for 10 to 12 minutes. Cool for 5 minutes on the baking sheet before transferring to a wire rack to cool completely. Store in an airtight container. The cookies freeze well.

*G*lorified ice-cream sandwiches. If you ever want to be valued, make these.

"The only emperor is the emperor of ice cream."
WALLACE STEVENS

Hot Latin Night

*H*ave you ever craved something hot and spicy on a hot summer evening? Perfectly natural. Your body is saying that if it can break out in a sweat, it will subsequently cool itself down. People in warm climates know all about this. So, on your own hot Latin night, try this dinner with a strong Spanish accent.

Paella, with its riotous colors and varied flavors, is a sure crowd-pleaser. It is also great fun to eat because of the surprise ingredients hidden in the rice: squid, sausage, lobster, shrimp, clams, and beans. The unaccustomed dusky color comes from the squid ink, which provides a rich background for the succulent ingredients and imparts an inspired flavor. This glorious Spanish dish is especially welcome when preceded by a chilled avocado soup, washed down with lots of icy sangría, and is accompanied by the refreshing orange salad.

I have a theory that conversation becomes more animated if guests are partaking of fiery food. If I am right, I'd say that's the best reason to serve this spicy dinner.

ORDER OF PREPARATION

*A*lthough the paella has a long list of ingredients, there are only a few simple steps to preparing it. Most of the menu can be done in advance. Start the night before by making the sangría, garlic sauce, ice cream, and cookies. Before your friends

Paella Negra—an inspired update of a classic dish

arrive, make the avocado soup and chill it for at least 30 minutes. To cope with the timing of the paella, allow 30 minutes to assemble the casserole, either before your guests arrive (it can sit for an hour or so unrefrigerated) or enlist a friend or two to help. It takes 40 minutes to cook. While it is cooking, drink some sangría, make the orange salad, and set the table.

Wine suggestion: In addition to or in place of the sangría, try a fresh Vinho Verde from Portugal, a light summertime quaffer, with a slight spritz.

*I*cy cold sangría can easily make one forget the "dog days" of summer. Unfortunately, this lovely Spanish summer drink was over-commercialized and bottled, giving it a bad name. Homemade, unadulterated sangría, mixed with fresh summer fruits, is delicious.

Make plenty. It slides down easily and quenches the thirst that comes with eating the spicy paella.

SANGRÍA
SERVES 6

2 bottles (48 ounces) full-bodied, dry Spanish red wine
1/3 cup freshly squeezed orange juice
1/4 cup Grand Marnier, or any orange-flavored liqueur

2 tablespoons sugar
2 cups club soda or mineral water
Ice cubes
GARNISH
  Orange and lemon slices
  Tart green apple slices
  Peach or nectarine slices

In a large pitcher, mix together the first 4 ingredients. Cover and refrigerate for several hours or overnight. Just before serving, add the club soda and plenty of ice cubes. Serve very cold garnished with a slice of fruit.

ICED AVOCADO-CUCUMBER SOUP
SERVES 6

3 tablespoons unsalted butter
1 medium-size onion, minced
3 garlic cloves, peeled and pressed
5 cups chicken broth, preferably homemade
2 large ripe avocados, peeled and pitted (enough to yield 2 cups pulp)

1 cup tomato sauce, homemade, bottled, or canned
1/4 teaspoon ground cumin
1/2 cup heavy cream
  Salt and freshly ground black pepper to taste
1 large cucumber, peeled, seeded, and cubed

In a soup pot over medium heat, melt the butter. Add the onion and garlic and cook until tender. Add the chicken broth and bring to a boil. Lower the heat and simmer for 10 minutes. Transfer the mixture to a blender or food processor and add avocados, tomato sauce, and cumin. Purée until smooth. Transfer to a bowl and cool; then cover and refrigerate. Before serving, stir in the cream and season with salt and pepper; then stir in the chopped cucumber.

TO RIPEN AN AVOCADO: To hasten the ripening of the rock-hard avocados found in most markets, place in a brown paper bag or wrap in paper and leave at room temperature overnight. If the avocados are very hard, it may take them two days to ripen by this method. If you really have your wits about you (and who does when it comes to these details), you will buy this one item well in advance of using it.

PAELLA NEGRA WITH GARLIC SAUCE

SERVES 6

6 cups fish broth
(preferably homemade)
or bottled clam juice

½ teaspoon saffron threads

1 pound squid, cleaned
and cut into rings
(Reserve approximately
½ cup of the ink.)

½ cup dry red wine

2 whole chicken cutlets, cut
into ½-inch cubes

4 chicken thighs, cut in half
Salt and freshly ground
black pepper to taste

⅓ cup olive oil

2 garlic cloves, peeled and
minced

1 large onion, finely
chopped

½ teaspoon crushed red
pepper

1 medium-size sweet yellow
pepper, finely chopped

3 cups short-grain rice

1 pound shrimp, shelled
and deveined with tails
left on

12 to 16 littleneck clams,
scrubbed well

1 pound hot, hard Spanish
chorizo or Italian
pepperoni, sliced

1 pound fresh tomatoes,
peeled, cored, and cut
into wedges, or 1 14½-
ounce can tomatoes,
drained and coarsely
chopped

1 cup fresh or frozen lima
beans

1 1½-pound lobster

¼ cup pimiento, cut into
thin strips
Finely chopped fresh
parsley
Lemon wedges
Garlic Sauce (recipe
follows)

Traditionally, paella is cooked on top of the stove in a large pan, a paetella, from which the dish takes its name. Here it is cooked in a large casserole in the oven. For authentic flavor and texture, it is essential to use short-grain rice. But you may vary this recipe as you wish. Add other vegetables or shellfish from the alternate list. Just be sure to keep the basic proportions the same.

Before starting, make sure you have an 18 × 24-inch casserole, roasting pan, or paella pan.

Preheat the oven to 350° F.

Bring the broth to a simmer in a saucepan. Dissolve the saffron in the broth and keep simmering until ready to use.

Using a wooden spoon, break the squid sacs into a sieve over a bowl. Mix the ink that comes through with the red wine. (If you don't want to do this, ask your fishmonger for approximately ½ cup of ink.) Set aside.

Sprinkle the chicken pieces with salt and pepper. In a large skillet, heat the oil, add the chicken in batches, and brown over medium-high heat until golden. Remove to a warm platter and cover to keep juicy.

Add the garlic, onion, crushed red pepper, and yellow pepper and cook over low heat, stirring frequently, until the vegetables are soft but not brown. Add the rice and cook until it is opaque and slightly golden, stirring with a wooden spoon. Next add the simmering broth along with the mixture of wine and squid ink.

Stir to loosen any brown bits on the bottom of the pan. Cover and simmer for 10 minutes. Rub a large casserole or paella pan or two small ones with olive oil. Put half of the partially cooked rice and broth into the casseroles. Tuck half the uncooked shellfish (shrimp, clams, and squid), chorizo slices, cooked chicken, tomato wedges, and lima beans into the rice. Spoon the remaining rice and broth over these. Arrange the remaining ingredients on top, pushing the shrimp, clams, and sausage into the

FOR A MODIFIED FIESTA ATMOSPHERE: String decorative paper garlands (available at party supply stores) from the trees around the dining area. Flaring torches and glowing candles complete the picture.

*S*imilar to aïoli, the French garlic mayonnaise.

rice. Cover with a lid or loosely with aluminum foil. Bake for 30 minutes. If too dry, add additional *boiling* broth.

While the paella is cooking, bring a large pot of salted water to a rapid boil. Plunge the lobster, head first, into the boiling water. Cover the pot, return to a boil, and boil for 12 to 15 minutes for a 1½- to 2-pound lobster. When done remove from the pot with tongs and drain well.

Remove the cover from the paella and bake until the rice is fluffy and all the liquid has been absorbed, about 10 to 15 minutes. Arrange the cooked lobster on top, and let rest for 10 minutes before serving.

Decorate with the pimiento strips, parsley, and lemon wedges. To serve, split the lobster and cut the tail, claws, and body into pieces.

Pass the Garlic Sauce at the table.

GARLIC SAUCE

MAKES 1 CUP

8 to 10 garlic cloves,
  smashed and peeled
½ teaspoon salt
1 large egg yolk

1 tablespoon freshly
  squeezed lemon juice
1 cup olive oil

In a food processor or blender, combine the garlic, salt, egg yolk, and lemon juice. Process until smooth. With the machine on, gradually dribble in the olive oil until the mixture is as thick as mayonnaise. Transfer to a bowl, cover tightly, and refrigerate until ready to serve.

ENSALADA VALENCIANA

SERVES 6

4 to 5 navel oranges
1 medium-size red onion,
  peeled and sliced paper-
  thin
¾ cup (approximately 20)
  whole pitted cured black
  olives
DRESSING
½ cup olive oil

2 garlic cloves, peeled and
  pressed through a garlic
  press
½ teaspoon paprika
½ teaspoon salt
  A good dash of Tabasco
  sauce
½ teaspoon ground cumin
¼ cup freshly squeezed
  lemon juice

Peel and slice the oranges. Discard any seeds. Alternate the oranges with the red onion slices on a serving platter in an overlapping pattern. Scatter the olives over all.

In a small bowl, whisk together the dressing ingredients. Pour the dressing over the salad, distributing it evenly. Let stand at room temperature for 20 to 30 minutes before serving.

An interesting and refreshing combination, this orange and red onion salad tames and complements the spicy paella.

Piña Colada Ice Cream with Blueberries

SERVES 6

1 cup canned coconut
 cream
8 large egg yolks
1 cup plus 2 tablespoons
 sugar
1½ cups cubed fresh
 pineapple
¼ cup dark rum

2 cups heavy cream (see
 Note)
1 cup blueberries
 (optional)
GARNISH
 Blueberries
 Mint sprigs

In a heavy saucepan, bring the coconut cream to a simmer. Meanwhile, in a large bowl, beat the egg yolks with 1 cup of the sugar until pale and thick. Gradually beat the hot coconut cream into the sugar and egg yolk mixture. Return the mixture to the saucepan and cook over low heat for 3 to 4 minutes, stirring constantly until the custard thickens. (Do not boil or the custard will curdle.) Cool by setting the pan in a large bowl filled with ice.

In a food processor or blender, purée the pineapple with the rum and the remaining 2 tablespoons of sugar.

Fold the pineapple mixture and heavy cream into the custard. Freeze following the manufacturer's instructions for your ice-cream maker. Soften slightly in the refrigerator before serving.

Garnish with several tablespoons of blueberries and a mint sprig.

NOTE: For the calorie-watchers I have successfully substituted plain yogurt for the heavy cream.

Set your table in "Hot Latin" colors, and use any assortment of Mexican platters or decorations—especially brightly colored paper streamers.

Pecan Sugar Cookies

MAKES TWENTY-FOUR 2-INCH COOKIES

¾ cup (about 4 ounces)
 pecans
½ cup sugar
1 cup all-purpose flour
 Pinch of salt

¼ cup (½ stick) unsalted
 butter
¼ cup vegetable shortening
1 large egg, lightly beaten
 Confectioners' sugar

A cookie is only good if you can eat it by the dozen. These are light and crisp and enhance rather than overpower summer fruits or ice creams. With a food processor they take only seconds to make.

In a food processor or blender, grind the pecans. Add the sugar and then flour and salt. Work in the butter, shortening, and egg until a dough forms. Gather the dough into a ball, wrap in plastic wrap, and refrigerate for 30 minutes or until firm.

Preheat the oven to 300° F. On a lightly floured surface, roll the dough out to a thickness of ¼ inch. Cut into cookies with a 2-inch fluted cutter and bake on an ungreased baking sheet for 20 to 25 minutes or until just brown around the edges. Cool on a wire rack. Dust with confectioners' sugar before serving.

These cookies will keep crisp for several days in an airtight container and may be frozen.

Midsummer's Night

M·e·n·u

YELLOW SQUASH SOUP
WITH BASIL CREAM

·

SOUTHERN FRIED
GREEN TOMATOES

·

CORN PUDDING

·

CREPINETTES

·

GINGER SHORTCAKE
WITH PEACHES AND CREAM

*D*esigned to complement the mellow glow of a fine summer evening, this dinner has a warm, sunny air about it. In fact, it is mostly yellow. Informal and unpretentious (even the crepinettes, despite the French name, are simple fare and easy to prepare), the menu depends, to a marked degree, on the freshness and quality of the local fruits and vegetables you select. This golden repast is far from bland. The squash soup is set off with basil cream. The crepinettes are sparked with a mixture of fresh herbs and spices, and the peaches and cream accompany a shortcake enlivened by fresh ginger.

To avoid spending excessive time in a hot kitchen, plan on preparing most of the dishes in advance—early in the cool of the day. Only the corn pudding and the tomatoes need be made in the hour before dinner. Incidentally, the making of homemade sausage is not as hard as it might sound to someone who has not tried it, especially since I have omitted the step of stuffing the meat into casings.

ORDER OF PREPARATION

*M*ake the sausages up to a day in advance and wrap them in the chard leaves. On the morning of the dinner, prepare the shortcakes, and while they are baking, make the soup.

Prepare the peaches but keep them separate until you assemble the shortcakes. Make the corn pudding 1 hour before you want to sit down. Gently heat up the soup and make the basil cream. While the corn pudding is cooking, make the tomatoes and the crepinettes—the first in the frying pan, the second on the grill. Unless you are adept at being in two places at once, it's good to have someone on hand who can watch one or the other. Later, while friends relax with coffee, whip the cream and assemble the shortcakes. Don't forget the garnish.

Wine suggestion: A young Gamay would liven the evening.

YELLOW SQUASH SOUP WITH BASIL CREAM

SERVES 6

4 tablespoons unsalted butter
1 medium-size onion, finely chopped
4 cups sliced yellow squash (about 1½ pounds)
1 cup finely chopped carrots
2½ cups defatted chicken broth, preferably homemade

1 cup half-and-half
1 teaspoon salt
   Freshly ground white pepper to taste

Basil Cream (recipe follows)

GARNISH
   Nasturtium blossoms

A delicate summer soup the color of sunflowers—the perfect solution for the avalanche of summer squash coming from your garden.

Melt the butter in a heavy, deep saucepan over low heat. Add the onion, cover, and cook until the onion is limp but not brown, about 10 minutes. Add the yellow squash and carrots and stir to coat with the butter. Cover and cook undisturbed for 10 to 15 minutes or until soft.

Bring the chicken broth to a boil and add to the vegetables. Simmer, uncovered, for 15 minutes more or until the vegetables are tender but retain some firmness. Remove to a food processor, blender, or food mill and purée to a smooth consistency. Return the mixture to a clean saucepan. Pour in the half-and-half and season with salt and pepper. If the soup is too sweet, add a little dry white wine or lemon juice to taste. Bring to a simmer over low heat before serving.

Ladle the hot soup into warm individual serving bowls. Add a teaspoon of Basil Cream and swirl it through the soup. Serve immediately, decorating each bowl with a nasturtium blossom.

BASIL CREAM

MAKES ABOUT 1 CUP

½ cup fresh basil   ½ cup heavy cream

While the soup is heating, finely chop the basil in a food processor or blender. Add the heavy cream, a little at a time, as if making mayonnaise until a thick sauce is formed.

"Beautiful Soup!
Who cares for fish, game, or any other dish?
Who would not give all else for two
pennyworth only of beautiful soup?"
LEWIS CARROLL

Yellow squash soup combined with basil—as joyous to taste as it is to behold

· · · · · · ❁ · · · · · ·

SOUTHERN FRIED GREEN TOMATOES

SERVES 6

1 cup stone-ground white
   cornmeal (available in
   specialty food shops)
6 green tomatoes, cut into
   thick slices
2 tablespoons olive oil
4 tablespoons unsalted
   butter

½ cup firmly packed dark
   brown sugar
¼ cup chopped fresh
   coriander or Italian
   parsley
   Freshly ground black
   pepper to taste

Dip the tomato slices into the cornmeal, coating them well on both sides. Heat the oil and butter in a heavy skillet. Add the tomato slices in one layer (you will need to fry them in several batches). Sprinkle the tops with brown sugar and sauté over medium heat for 2 to 3 minutes. Turn the slices and sprinkle with more brown sugar. Continue cooking until the sugar caramelizes. Watch carefully so they do not brown. Turn once more to caramelize the other side. Remove to a warm platter and sprinkle with the coriander and a few grindings of black pepper.

OPPOSITE: My grandmother makes this sweet and spicy dish at the end of summer with the supply of unripened tomatoes from her garden. Delicious with fried bacon and corn muffins for breakfast, it's also a perfect accompaniment to the crepinettes.

So sweet it could almost be dessert.

CORN PUDDING

SERVES 6

6 ears fresh corn, shucked (about 3 cups)
6 large eggs, beaten lightly
1½ cups milk
1½ cups heavy cream
2 teaspoons crushed anise seed
2 teaspoons salt
½ teaspoon cayenne pepper
1 bunch scallions, minced
3 tablespoons unsalted butter, melted
¼ cup shredded Asiago cheese

Preheat the oven to 350° F.

Using a sharp knife, cut the kernels of corn from the cobs into a mixing bowl. Set aside.

In a separate bowl, beat the eggs until smooth. Add the milk, heavy cream, anise seed, salt, cayenne, scallions, and melted butter. Stir in the corn until the mixture is combined well.

Pour the pudding into a well-buttered 6-cup soufflé dish. Sprinkle the cheese over the top. Set the soufflé dish in a large roasting pan and pour in boiling water until it reaches halfway up the side of the soufflé dish. Bake the pudding for 55 to 60 minutes or until the center is just firm. Cover loosely with aluminum foil if the top is browning too quickly. Serve warm.

This recipe was contributed by Bruce Aidells, of Aidells Sausage Company in Kensington, California, a fabulous sausage maker and chef.

CREPINETTES

SERVES 6

2 pounds pork butt (from the loin or belly), coarsely ground or finely chopped with 20 percent pork fat
1 pound fresh spinach, blanched, drained thoroughly, and chopped, or 1 10-ounce package frozen chopped spinach, thawed and drained
2 shallots, finely chopped
1 garlic clove, peeled and minced
2 tablespoons minced fresh parsley
½ teaspoon dried tarragon
¼ teaspoon dried sage
¼ teaspoon dried thyme
2 teaspoons coarse salt, hand-ground if possible (see Note)
2 teaspoons sugar
2 teaspoons freshly ground black pepper
½ teaspoon ground allspice
¼ cup Madeira or brandy
2 tablespoons chopped fresh herbs, such as tarragon, thyme, oregano, and basil
12 to 14 large fresh Swiss chard leaves, preferably the red-veined "Rhubarb" variety, well washed
Olive oil

Mix the pork thoroughly with the spinach and all the seasonings, using your hands. Moisten your hands and mold the sausage meat into 3-ounce oval patties. You will get about 12 patties.

RUBY GREENS: Swiss chard is a real garden champion. Plant it in the spring and it will provide you with vitamin-rich greens late into the fall. When all else is gone, chard will be standing—in glowing health. "Rhubarb" is the variety with red stems and red-veined leaves. It is a beautiful plant with many uses.

Cut the stems from the Swiss chard leaves. Bring 2 quarts of water to a simmer. Blanch several leaves at a time, removing them just as they soften. Drain and pat dry. Wrap 1 Swiss chard leaf (not too tightly) around each sausage patty. Shape each into a neat package and place on a platter. Continue until you have used all the chard leaves and sausage. Cover and refrigerate for 30 minutes. Brush all over with olive oil and grill over moderate coals for 15 to 20 minutes, turning frequently.

NOTE: Natural rock or sea salts are available at most gourmet or health food stores. Large irregular crystals taste better, so put them in whole. When you bite into the crepinettes the little pockets of salt crystals will enhance the flavor of the sausage.

GINGER SHORTCAKE WITH PEACHES AND CREAM

SERVES 6

SHORTCAKES
- 2 tablespoons peeled and finely grated fresh ginger
- 3 tablespoons sugar
- 2 cups plus 1 tablespoon all-purpose flour
- 2 teaspoons baking powder
- ½ teaspoon salt
- 10 tablespoons unsalted butter, chilled and cut into small pieces
- ⅔ cup milk

PEACHES AND CREAM
- 4 to 5 large peaches
- 1 tablespoon freshly squeezed lemon juice
- ¼ cup honey
- 2 tablespoons Grand Marnier
- Grated rind of 1 orange
- 2 cups whipping cream

GARNISH
- Mint leaves
- Candied ginger sliced thin
- Blueberries

Served with cream, any fresh ripe peach is sublime. But, for sheer sensual beauty, try to find the somewhat esoteric white peach, smeared with glowing crimson where the flesh surrounds the pit.

Preheat the oven to 375° F.

To make the shortcakes, mix the ginger, sugar, and 1 tablespoon of the flour together in a small bowl. Set aside.

Sift the 2 cups of flour, baking powder, and salt together. Cut the butter into the dry ingredients with a fork or pastry blender or in the bowl of a food processor until the texture resembles oatmeal. Add the ginger mixture and mix well.

Add the milk. Mix until the mixture just holds together. Turn the dough onto a lightly floured surface and knead 10 or 15 times or until smooth. Use a lightly floured rolling pin to roll the dough to a thickness of 1 inch. Cut out 6 biscuits with a lightly floured 3-inch-round cutter. Bake on an ungreased baking sheet for 12 to 15 minutes or until lightly brown.

Slice the peaches and toss them with the lemon juice in a nonmetallic bowl.

In a small saucepan, over low heat, melt the honey with the Grand Marnier. Pour over the peaches, add the orange rind, and toss.

Beat the whipping cream until stiff.

To serve, split each biscuit in half. Put the bottom halves on individual dessert plates. Distribute the peaches and syrup over the biscuits. Add a dollop of whipped cream and top with the remaining biscuit. Put more whipped cream on top and garnish with mint leaves, thin slices of candied ginger, and a few blueberries.

The pick of the crop

Pick-of-the-Crop Dinner

M·e·n·u

CORN AND LIMA BEAN CHOWDER
·
GRILLED EGGPLANT AND SMOKED
MOZZARELLA SANDWICHES
·
MIXED GARDEN GRILL
·
SALSA RANCHERA
·
GRILLED CORN TORTILLAS
·
CANDIED WALNUTS

A moment comes at summer's high point when roadside farm stands and home gardens together provide a bounty almost impossible to contain. It is indisputably the *vegetable* moment, the perfect time to ransack the home garden for all it's worth. This is a dinner I have conceived to celebrate this time of plenty in our backyards. It is a dinner that celebrates some old American deities: thrift (what we do not pay for but have produced on our own has a special

ABOVE: Katie Smith passes judgment on my chowder. I think it's OK.

appeal) and convenience (gather your ingredients from your own well-tended plot of earth and pay no visit to the greengrocer's today). I like to see how much of a meal I can prepare straight out of the garden and without heating up the stove. Freshness, informality, and the out-of-doors are the keynotes on this occasion. Harvest the vegetables the same day as your dinner. In the evening, cook everything outside over a large grill. Wash down the vegetables and fiery salsa with lots of beer or white wine. This is, incidentally, a meal without meat, but it is not the omission of meat that is the point; it is the inclusion of so much else that is begging for a place at our table.

This dinner should be eaten in stages as it comes off the grill. It is not a formal sit-down affair and guests need not eat the courses in any particular order. Sit down over dessert as the last of the coals die down.

ORDER OF PREPARATION

*I*n the afternoon, scrape the corn and shell the limas for the chowder. Slice the vegetables and marinate them in individual bowls. Skewer the shallots and tomatillos. Weight down the eggplant slices. Slice the cheese, cover, and refrigerate.

While the coals are heating, make the chowder. Keep it warm or take it outside and reheat it in a heavy cast-iron casserole over the glowing coals. Serve it in over-size mugs to your friends as they arrive.

Make the salsa.

A word on order around the grill: Organization in this area can greatly affect the disposition of the cook as well as the general success of the barbecue ritual. Set up a small work area next to the grill to hold all the items to be cooked, as well as tools, marinade, and olive oil. Have a large platter ready for the cooked vegetables as they come off the grill. On a separate table set out eating utensils (plates, napkins, mugs, etc.), salsa, and warm tortillas.

Have a guest toast the walnuts with the sugar while you prepare the ice cream, brandy, and figs. If you can get them, white kadota and brown turkey figs are pretty when arranged together on fresh fig, grape, or maple leaves.

Wine suggestion: Serve with an amber-style, highly hopped beer, or a youthful, berry-like Zinfandel.

GRILLING HINTS: Make sure the grill surface is clean and oiled. The average fire will take 30 to 40 minutes to reach the proper temperature, so give yourself plenty of time. The ideal time to begin the grilling is when the coals are covered with a light gray ash around the outer edges. A thick well-packed fire is hotter than a thin layer of coals spread over the same surface. Food to be grilled should be at room temperature.

CORN AND LIMA BEAN CHOWDER

SERVES 6

1 cup finely chopped onion
1 cup finely chopped celery
1 teaspoon chopped fresh
  thyme or ¼ teaspoon dried
  thyme
2 tablespoons unsalted butter
4 cups chicken stock,
  preferably homemade
1 cup diced red new potatoes

4 cups corn kernels, scraped
  from garden-fresh corn if
  possible
2 cups lima beans, fresh, if
  possible
1 cup half-and-half
  Salt and freshly ground
  white pepper to taste
GARNISH
  Chopped chives

In a saucepan, sauté the onion, celery, and thyme in butter until crisp-tender. Meanwhile, bring chicken stock to a simmer in a soup pot; add potatoes and cook until just tender.

In a blender or food processor, purée 2 cups of the corn kernels with a little of the hot chicken stock until smooth. Add the blended corn, remaining corn kernels, lima beans, and sautéed vegetables to the soup pot. Simmer for 10 minutes. Stir in the half-and-half and season with salt and pepper. Garnish with chopped chives.

GRILLED EGGPLANT AND SMOKED MOZZARELLA SANDWICHES

SERVES 6

2 large unpeeled purple
  eggplants, sliced into
  ¼-inch-thick rounds
  Salt

1 pound smoked
  mozzarella, or fresh
  buffalo mozzarella, thinly
  sliced
½ cup olive oil

Sprinkle the eggplant slices liberally with salt and layer them in a stainless steel colander. Cover with plastic wrap and weight down with a heavy weight, like an unopened 5-pound sack of flour or sugar. Put a large bowl under the colander to collect the water. Let stand for at least 30 minutes. Drain and pat dry.

Brush the slices generously on both sides with olive oil and grill on one side for 3 to 5 minutes. Turn the eggplant. Place a layer of cheese on the cooked side of half the eggplant slices and top with the remaining eggplant slices, cooked side down. Continue grilling both sides of the "sandwiches" until the eggplant is soft and the cheese runny. Brush with more oil, if necessary.

"Of all the items in a menu, soup is that which exacts the most delicate perfection and the strictest attention, for on the first impression it gives to the dinner the success of the rest of the meal must depend."
ESCOFFIER

To remove their bitterness, the thick slices of eggplant must be drained of excess moisture.

GRILLING PARAPHERNALIA: Use *long-handled* everything to keep the fire from singeing the hairs on your arms. I strongly suggest a basting brush, fork, tongs (spring-loaded), spatula (angled). Have on hand a spray bottle filled with water to control the flames.

The harvest grilling

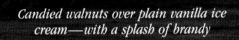
Candied walnuts over plain vanilla ice cream—with a splash of brandy

*B*ig is out. Small is in. Serve this array of Lilliputian vegetables grilled over grapevine clippings or chips. Add herb bundles of rosemary or fennel if you want an even fuller aromatic bouquet. Choose vegetables of a similar diminutive size to keep grilling times roughly the same.

MIXED GARDEN GRILL

SERVES 6

12 "baby" summer squash, yellow crookneck, regular and Gold Rush zucchini, or white and yellow pattypan squash

12 "baby" eggplant, Japanese (purple) and "Easter" (white) eggplant, cut lengthwise into ¼-inch-thick slices

8 sweet red, yellow, or green peppers, seeded and cut in quarters

12 elephant garlic cloves, skins left on

12 okra, slit lengthwise and seeded

18 each shallots and bay leaves, threaded on bamboo skewers (see Note)

18 each tomatillos and bay leaves, threaded on bamboo skewers (see Note)

12 leeks, trimmed and cleaned

2 cups olive oil

1 cup dry white wine

6 garlic cloves, smashed and peeled

½ cup finely chopped fresh rosemary

Arrange the sliced vegetables in large roasting pans, keeping similar types together.
Combine the oil, wine, garlic, and rosemary in a bowl. Pour the marinade over the vegetables. Cover and let stand for at least 30 minutes. Turn the vegetables once.
Over moderate coals, grill the vegetables until just tender turning once and basting frequently with the marinade. Grilling time will depend on the vegetables. The shallots and tomatillos take longest so cook them first.
NOTE: To avoid scorching the ends of the bamboo skewers, soak them in warm water for 30 minutes before using.

*S*erve this uncooked tomato sauce along with the grilled vegetables and tortillas. Spoon over the eggplant sandwiches. Do not overblend the salsa: It should be chunky in texture. Although this can be made hours in advance, it is best made just before serving, for it quickly loses its fresh tomato flavor and the bite of the coriander.

SALSA RANCHERA

MAKES ABOUT 1 CUP

2 garlic cloves, peeled

½ medium-size onion

6 serrano chiles

2 medium-size ripe tomatoes

⅓ cup freshly squeezed lime juice

½ teaspoon salt, preferably coarse ground

1 small bunch fresh coriander, finely chopped

Finely chop the first 4 ingredients by hand or in a food processor. There is no need to seed the chiles or tomatoes. Mix together in a bowl and add the lime juice and salt. Sprinkle the coriander over the sauce and serve.

GRILLED CORN TORTILLAS

SERVES 6

12 6- to 8-inch round fresh corn tortillas
(Use locally made tortillas if possible.)

Grill the tortillas for 3 to 4 seconds on each side over moderate coals. Wrap in a towel to keep warm.

CANDIED WALNUTS

MAKES 2 CUPS

2 cups sugar   *2 cups walnut halves*

Toss the walnuts with the sugar and spread them on a sheet of heavy-duty aluminum foil over the grill. Turn frequently until the sugar has melted and the nuts are toasty.

Sprinkle the nuts over dishes of vanilla ice cream splashed with brandy.

"I won't eat anything that has intelligent life, but I'd gladly eat a network executive or a politician."
MARTY FELDMAN

FALL

Indian Summer

*T*hough culled from far-off shores, this is a dinner to crown one of those warm, burnished string of fall days we know in this country as Indian Summer. Here is a late opportunity to use the grill, eat outdoors, and even enjoy a last watermelon, all of summer's sweetness stored in its pink flesh. The piquancy and fire of these dishes nicely offsets the whispers of cold circulating in the evening air. The menu is East Indian in inspiration, but I have looked to northern Africa for the couscous salad and to the Mideast for the hummus and poppadums.

I love Indian food. Of all cuisines in the ethnic category, it is my favorite. Its aromatic spices and haunting flavors and textures enthrall my senses. To someone whose early understanding of the directive ''adjust the seasoning'' consisted of a dim idea about adding salt and pepper, the varied and subtle world of India's spices and herbs came as a revelation. And, besides, who can resist a style of cooking that relies so heavily on all those delightful little side dishes?

People are hesitant to cook Indian food at home. They think the food is going to be too ''hot,'' and that the ingredients will be unavailable. Both are misapprehensions. The cuisine is *spicy,* not hot. As to availability of raw materials, most of the ''exotic'' ingredients already reside on our pantry shelves or are regulars at our local markets. It is only the combinations that are unexpected and new.

ORDER OF PREPARATION

*F*or this meal, organization is everything; there are lots of little jobs to be done. Get most of the work for this menu out of the way in advance. The night before (or several hours ahead) you can make the cookies, make the marinade (or marinades), and marinate the meat. You can also prepare the hummus, relishes, and dipping sauce. Each of these takes only minutes with a blender or food processor.

An hour before your guests arrive make the couscous and cut up the vegetables for the grill. Fry the poppadums just before your friends begin to arrive. Start the grill about 30 minutes before you wish to grill the kabobs. Enlist someone to handle the grilling of the kabobs and vegetables while you prepare the table. (Of course, in this way friends can also share in all triumphs—and disasters.) Cut up the watermelon just before serving it with the ginger cookies.

Wine suggestions: Try a refreshing Zinfandel or a dry but fruity Chardonnay. If you prefer beer, look for beer that is hopped, not malted. Try the Thailand brewed Singha, quite light in alcohol, or bittersweet Corona. If you can't find these, the light and versatile Danish Carlsburg is another good choice.

POPPADUMS

SERVES 6

2 to 3 cups peanut oil

1 can or box (approximately 20) poppadums

Heat the oil in a large skillet until very hot but not smoking. Use a tong to slide the poppadums singly into the hot oil. Turn immediately and fry for 3 to 5 *seconds.* Poppadums brown very quickly so watch carefully. Drain on paper towels. Repeat with the remaining poppadums. Serve at room temperature or heat in a moderate oven for 5 minutes. Use the poppadums to scoop up the hummus.

*T*hese appealing wafers should replace potato chips as a staple in your pantry. They are inexpensive and a lot more fun. When cooked they puff up to twice their size, resembling large exotic blooms or lotus petals. Poppadums are made from lentil flour, which has a slightly sweet, provocative taste, and they come either plain or spiced. I like the plain best.

HUMMUS

SERVES 6

3 cups cooked dried or canned chick-peas
6 garlic cloves, peeled and finely chopped
½ cup tahini (sesame seed paste)

½ cup freshly squeezed lemon juice
2 teaspoons freshly ground black pepper

Cook the dried chick-peas according to the package directions. Drain, reserving the liquid. (If canned chick-peas are used, reserve the liquid and rinse the peas under cold water.) In a food processor or blender, roughly chop the garlic and chick-peas together. Add the tahini, lemon juice, and pepper. Purée, adding the reserved liquid to make a smooth, thick spread. Transfer to a serving bowl, cover, and refrigerate until ready to serve.

*W*hat this Middle Eastern spread lacks in appearance it makes up for in flavor.

Boti kabobs served on a copper plate

Hummus, coriander-mint relish,
pungent peanut sauce, and tomato relish
—four intensely flavored dipping sauces

*B*oti kabobs, a favorite street food in Delhi, are cubes of marinated meat or fish skewered and grilled over hot coals. Rubbed well with their exotic spiced marinades, kabobs are a good choice for the last of the year's outdoor meals; they have do-ahead appeal (marinate and leave in the refrigerator overnight) and take only minutes on the grill.

Although it is the marinade that distinguishes a good kabob, the relishes and dipping sauce are every bit as important. I have chosen three marinades and three accompaniments, so you can mix and match. Grill the kabobs over hot charcoal or mesquite. Add hickory chips or fruit woods, which have first been soaked in water, or toss branches of bay laurel onto the fire (if you are lucky enough to live where it grows) to add an unusual aromatic flavor to the meat.

BOTI KABOBS

Allow ¼ to ½ pound of meat for each person.

Thread 3 to 4 pieces of meat onto a skewer. Arrange the skewers in a shallow dish and pour the marinade over them. Cover with plastic wrap and refrigerate for at least 1 hour or overnight.

Grill over hot coals, brushing with the marinade and turning until nicely charred on all sides, about 8 to 10 minutes.

MARINADE FOR LAMB, PORK, OR CHICKEN

FOR 1½ POUNDS OF MEAT

1½ cups soy sauce
1 tablespoon molasses
¾ cup hot water
¾ cup chunky peanut butter, made fresh if possible

1 garlic clove, peeled
⅛ teaspoon crushed red pepper, or to taste
Juice of 1 lemon

Combine all the ingredients in a food processor or blender, and process until you have a smooth paste.

MARINADE FOR BEEF, PORK, OR CHICKEN

FOR 1½ POUNDS OF MEAT

2 teaspoons ground cumin
2 teaspoons ground coriander
1 tablespoon minced fresh ginger
2 garlic cloves, peeled

2 tablespoons Thai or Oriental fish sauce (available in Oriental markets)
⅓ cup water
2 tablespoons peanut oil

Combine all the ingredients in a food processor or electric blender and process until well blended.

MARINADE FOR FISH, SHELLFISH, OR CHICKEN

FOR 1½ POUNDS OF MEAT

1 tablespoon minced fresh ginger
3 garlic cloves, peeled
1 tablespoon olive oil
1 tablespoon vegetable oil
½ teaspoon powdered dry mustard

1 small bunch fresh coriander (about 1 cup)
¼ cup chopped scallions
Juice of 1 lemon
Salt to taste

Combine all the ingredients in a food processor or electric blender, and process until well blended.

CORIANDER-MINT RELISH

MAKES ABOUT 2 CUPS

1/4 chopped onion
1 tablespoon minced fresh
  ginger
2 green chiles, seeded and
  chopped
1/4 sweet green pepper, cored,
  seeded, and chopped

1/4 cup fresh mint
1 small bunch fresh
  coriander
1 teaspoon sugar
1 teaspoon salt
2 tablespoons water
Juice of 2 limes

Put all the ingredients in a food processor or blender and blend just long enough to chop finely. Transfer to a bowl, cover, and refrigerate until ready to serve.

PUNGENT PEANUT SAUCE

MAKES 2½ CUPS

2 garlic cloves, peeled
1 small onion, chopped
1 cup peanuts, skins
  removed
2 tablespoons minced fresh
  ginger
1/4 cup peanut oil

1½ cups unsweetened coconut
  milk
2 tablespoons sugar
2 tablespoons soy sauce
Juice of 1 lemon

GARNISH
  Freshly grated coconut or
  chopped coriander

In a food processor or blender, purée the garlic, onion, peanuts, and ginger with the oil until you have a smooth paste. Add the remaining ingredients and mix well. Pour the sauce into a saucepan and simmer over low heat until thick, stirring frequently, about 3 to 4 minutes. Thin to desired consistency with more coconut milk or water. Garnish with grated coconut or chopped coriander.

NOTE: For a different taste, replace the peanuts in this recipe with brazil nuts or almonds.

TOMATO RELISH

MAKES ABOUT 2 CUPS

2 medium-size ripe
  tomatoes, cored and
  coarsely chopped
1 medium-size onion,
  coarsely chopped
1 teaspoon ground cumin

1 teaspoon salt
Freshly ground black
  pepper to taste
Juice of 1 lemon
1/4 cup olive oil

Combine all the ingredients in a nonmetallic serving bowl. Cover and refrigerate until ready to serve.

"**S**unset signaled the approach of dinner. A large cotton rug was unfolded in the courtyard. On this was spread a clean cotton sheet. Food was brought in on serving plates and placed in the center of the sheet. I always liked to carry in my favorite dishes, so I could look at them longer."
MADHUR JAFFREY
An Invitation to Indian Cooking

Delicate poppadums

Traditional couscous took a long time to prepare. It was steamed as part of a lengthy procedure in a two-part pot called a *couscoussier*. However, the new quick-cooking form can be prepared in a matter of minutes and is just as good as the old-fashioned type. The unique texture of the ground semolina evokes the exotic cuisine of North Africa and is a welcome departure from rice or pasta.

No dessert captures the spirit of the end of summer as perfectly as watermelon. This permeable fruit will soak up the flavors of liquor or wine. Vodka was the old college trick. But, for a more subtle taste, try drizzling a dry Riesling or Gewürztraminer over the bright red fruit.

GRILLED PEPPERS AND EGGPLANT

SERVES 6

6 small Japanese eggplants
2 each red, yellow, and green sweet peppers, stemmed, seeded, and cut into quarters

1 cup olive oil
Salt and freshly ground black pepper to taste

Prepare the grill.

Cut the eggplants up to the stem at ¼-inch intervals, and fan out the slices. Brush the vegetables all over with the olive oil and season with salt and pepper. Grill the vegetables for a few minutes on each side until tender.

COUSCOUS SALAD

SERVES 6

2 cups water
6 tablespoons unsalted butter
2 teaspoons cardamom seeds, 1 medium-size cinnamon stick, 2 bay leaves, tied together in cheesecloth
3 cups quick-cooking couscous
3 tablespoons peanut oil

1 medium-size onion, finely chopped
2 garlic cloves, peeled
¼ cup peeled and finely chopped fresh ginger
1 tablespoon salt
Freshly ground black pepper to taste
¼ cup chopped pistachio nuts or almonds
½ cup fresh parsley

Bring the water to a boil and add the butter and spice bag. Simmer until the butter melts. Place the couscous in a serving bowl and pour the broth over it. Stir gently, cover, and let stand for 5 minutes. Discard the bouquet garni.

Heat the oil in a saucepan and sauté the onion, garlic, and ginger for 2 to 3 minutes or until the onion is translucent and soft. Fold the mixture into the couscous along with the salt, pepper, nuts, and parsley. Serve warm or at room temperature.

WATERMELON IN WHITE WINE

SERVES 6

1 small red watermelon

1 bottle white wine

Cut the melon into ½-inch-thick triangles or wedges and let each guest pour on his or her own wine.

GINGER COOKIES

MAKES THIRTY-SIX 3-INCH COOKIES

1 cup (2 sticks) unsalted
    butter, softened
¼ cup packed light brown
    sugar
¼ cup granulated sugar
1 large egg yolk

1 tablespoon vanilla extract
1 cup all-purpose flour
¼ teaspoon salt
1 tablespoon ground ginger
    Granulated sugar for
    coating

A luscious watermelon paired with delicate, crisp cookies that are very simple to make

In a mixing bowl, cream the butter with the sugars until light and fluffy. Add the egg yolk and vanilla and blend thoroughly.

Sift together the flour, salt, and ginger. Gradually add the sifted dry ingredients to the creamed butter mixture, beating only to mix. Chill the mixture in the refrigerator for 10 to 15 minutes.

Lightly flour your hands and a work surface. Turn the chilled dough out onto the floured surface, press it into a cylinder about 2½ to 3 inches in diameter and 8 inches long. Wrap in plastic wrap and refrigerate for 1 hour.

To bake, preheat the oven to 350° F. With a very sharp knife slice the dough cylinder into ¼-inch-thick rounds. Dip one side of each cookie into the granulated sugar and place, sugar side up, about 2 inches apart on an ungreased baking sheet. Bake for 12 minutes or until the edges are golden brown. Remove to a wire rack to cool. Store in an airtight container. (These cookies don't freeze well.)

"**W**hen one has tasted watermelons, one knows what angels eat. It was not a Southern watermelon that Eve took; we know it because she repented."
MARK TWAIN

Crab Feast

*T*he platter-sized Dungeness crab of the West Coast arrives in fish markets throughout California in October and the inception of its long season marks the end of warm weather. Aptly named *Cancer magister,* this magnificent crustacean, orange to brick-red when cooked, often weighs in at about 2 pounds and will yield on an average one and a half cups of the sweetest, most succulent white meat imaginable. Here in Napa Valley the traditional way to celebrate the opening of crab season is the Crab Feast, a no-holds-barred affair where Dungeness enthusiasts crack and pick at the fresh crab crop on newspaper-strewn tables.

The best way I know to feast on crab is to incorporate this glory into a late Sunday supper. This is an easy finger-food menu (forks are needed only for the salad), and friends and family will revel in its appealing physicality. Buy the crabs cooked from your fishmonger; just make sure they are cooked on the day of the supper. (You can substitute the smaller Eastern blue crab for the Dungeness, though you will have to work harder to make a meal of it.) Avoid the supermarket crab, for you do not know when it was cooked. Before the feast, spread out the whole down-and-dirty operation on a plastic- or newspaper-covered table (preferably outdoors), provide wooden mallets and picks for cracking the crabs, paper painters' buckets for the shells, and lots and lots of napkins. There is a technique for cracking crabs, best learned by show-and-tell, but I have found that most people, unschooled in the finer points of technique, will find their own ways to get the delicate crab meat out of the shell.

ORDER OF PREPARATION

*T*he biscotti and tangerine sherbet can be made several days in advance. Both keep well. The *fougasse,* a yeast bread that goes stale quickly, is best made in the afternoon or late morning of the supper. The only dishes that should be prepared right before the feast are the pepper shrimp, gazpacho salad, and avocado salsa. Salsa likes to sit for about an hour to develop the best taste and the salad requires some chopping time. Make these at your leisure before people arrive. The shrimp takes only minutes to make, and its pungent smell will welcome your guests.

One virtue of this meal is an easy cleanup. When friends depart, just roll up the carnage in the newspapers and throw it all away.

Wine suggestion: Beer is perfect, but a chilled Johannisberg Riesling would also be great with the crab.

PEPPER SHRIMP

SERVES 6

2 pounds medium-size
  shrimp
½ teaspoon crushed red
  pepper
1 teaspoon cayenne pepper
1 teaspoon freshly ground
  black pepper
1 tablespoon chopped fresh
  thyme, or 1 teaspoon dried
  thyme
1 tablespoon chopped fresh
  rosemary, or 1 teaspoon
  dried rosemary

2 teaspoons chopped fresh
  oregano, or ¾ teaspoons
  dried oregano
¾ cup (1½ sticks) unsalted
  butter
2 garlic cloves, peeled and
  minced
1 teaspoon Worcestershire
  sauce
½ cup bottled clam juice
¼ cup beer
  Avocado Salsa (recipe
  follows)

I suppose these fiery shrimp belong in the popular Cajun-food category, although I first encountered them as a special treat that my mother brought home from her trips to Richmond. I would eat them slowly and carefully, savoring each hot, delicious mouthful.

Rinse the shrimp and pat them dry. Remove the "feet" if desired, but do not remove the shells.

In a small bowl combine the spices and herbs, and set aside. Melt ½ cup of the butter in a large skillet. When the foam subsides, add the garlic and sauté for 1 minute. Add the Worcestershire sauce and seasonings and mix well. Add the shrimp and cook over high heat for 2 minutes, stirring all the time with a wooden spoon. Remove from the heat and add the remaining butter cut into small pieces. Return to the heat and add the clam juice and beer, and cook and stir for 2 to 3 minutes more. Serve immediately with Avocado Salsa and lots of bread and beer. Everyone peels his own shrimp at the table, so have stacks of napkins and a shell bucket handy.

LEFT: The crusty steamed Dungeness crab posed against a fan-shaped fougasse

BELOW: A close look at the light, colorful, and refreshing gaspacho salad

RIGHT: Served on last week's funnies and accompanied by a trusty, much-needed pail, an October Fest not soon to be forgotten

This recipe was inspired by Cindy Pawlcyn, the chef at Mustard's Grill in Napa, California.

AVOCADO SALSA

MAKES 2½ CUPS

2 ripe avocados, peeled and
   cubed
½ medium-size bunch fresh
   coriander, finely chopped
2 scallions, minced
2 garlic cloves, peeled and
   minced

1 cup olive oil
⅓ cup freshly squeezed
   lemon juice
Salt and freshly ground
   black pepper to taste

Combine all the ingredients in a bowl and mix well. This is best done by hand —a food processor makes the salsa too mushy. Cover and let stand for 1 hour at room temperature before serving.

This recipe comes from the Model Bakery in St. Helena where its owner, Karen Mitchell, has made it famous. Delicious flavored with sage or parsley; irresistible with rosemary.

FOUGASSE WITH ROSEMARY

SERVES 6

1 ounce active dry yeast
1⅓ cups lukewarm water
¼ cup olive oil
5¼ cups all-purpose flour

¼ cup finely chopped fresh
   herbs (rosemary, sage, or
   parsley)
1 teaspoon salt
1 cup olive oil
1 tablespoon coarse salt

In a large mixing bowl, dissolve the yeast in ½ cup of the lukewarm water. Let it proof for 10 minutes. Add the olive oil, flour, herbs, salt, and remaining water to make a soft dough. Knead in an electric mixer with a dough hook or by hand for 5 minutes or until smooth and elastic, adding a little more flour to prevent sticking. Oil the same bowl, without washing, and turn the dough several times to coat it. Cover with a damp clean kitchen towel or plastic wrap and put in a warm place, away from drafts, to double in bulk, 1½ to 2 hours.

Punch down the dough, divide into two pieces, shape into two balls, and return the bowl. Cover with olive oil. Let rise for 20 to 30 minutes or until light.

Preheat the oven to 400° F.

Flatten each ball by hand onto a baking sheet to form large, flat circles ½ inch thick. Make 4 to 5 parallel slashes on each circle with a sharp knife to form a ladder or on a slight angle to form tree branches. Use your fingers to spread apart the slashes. Sprinkle with coarse salt.

Bake for 20 minutes or until golden brown. Brush the *fougasse* with oil again after baking.

STEAMED DUNGENESS CRAB

Place 4 whole cleaned and cracked Dungeness crabs, 2 to 2½ pounds each, in a steamer over boiling water and steam for 12 to 15 minutes. The crabs are done when they turn a bright orange or brick-red color. Serve cold with Avocado Salsa or homemade mayonnaise.

GAZPACHO SALAD

SERVES 6

VINAIGRETTE
¾ cup olive oil
¼ cup freshly squeezed
   lemon juice
¼ cup tomato juice (or use
   strained juice from
   reserved pulp)
2 teaspoons ground cumin
1 garlic clove, peeled and
   minced
¼ cup coarsely chopped fresh
   coriander
   Salt to taste

2 ripe tomatoes, cut in half,
   seeded, and cut into thin
   strips (Reserve the pulp
   and juice for the
   dressing.)

1 small red onion, peeled,
   cut in half lengthwise, and
   then sliced into thin strips
1 sweet red pepper, cored,
   seeded, and julienned
1 sweet yellow pepper, cored,
   seeded, and julienned
3 celery stalks, cut on the
   diagonal into ¼-inch
   pieces
1 cucumber, cut in half
   lengthwise, seeded, and
   cut into ¼-inch cubes
1 small jícama, peeled and
   julienned

Mix all the ingredients for the vinaigrette together in a bowl until the oil and lemon juice are thoroughly blended.

Toss the vegetables together in a large bowl with the Tomato-Cumin Vinaigrette. Let the salad sit, covered, at room temperature for up to 30 minutes to develop flavor.

Caught in Pacific waters from Alaska to California, these crabs have become a symbol of San Francisco's Fisherman's Wharf, where great mounds of them are sold precooked, whole or cracked. They are available between October and May and their delicate meat is pure crab heaven. Usually the fishmonger will cook, clean, and crack them for you, but this takes away some of the hands-on sport of the Crab Feast. For true aficionados, here are instructions for steaming at home.

"Anything can be a lodestar in a person's life, I suppose, and for some fortunates like me, the kitchen serves well. Often the real influence of a lodestar is half understood, or partly unsuspected, but with a little reflection it grows clear to me that kitchens have always played a mysterious part in my shaping."
M.F.K. FISHER
As They Were

A chocolate version of the delectable Italian biscotti, which is traditionally dipped in red wine or Grappa at the end of a meal. These cookies have a satisfying crunchy texture and a slightly bittersweet taste that you can't seem to get enough of.

CHOCOLATE BISCOTTI

MAKES 3 DOZEN COOKIES

6 ounces hazelnuts
3 large eggs, separated
1¼ cups sugar
½ cup (1 stick) unsalted butter
4 ounces unsweetened chocolate

½ teaspoon vanilla extract
3¼ cups all-purpose flour
½ teaspoon baking powder
1 large egg white, lightly beaten

Preheat the oven to 375° F. Spread the hazelnuts on a baking sheet and toast them in the oven for 5 to 8 minutes. Remove the nuts from the oven and, while they are still warm, wrap them in a clean dish towel. Let them steam for 1 to 2 minutes; then rub the nuts together vigorously in the cloth to remove as much of the skins as possible. Leave some of the nuts whole and then finely chop a quarter of the nuts and coarsely chop the rest. Lower the temperature to 350° F.

Melt the chocolate with the butter in the top of a double boiler, covered and set over hot water over moderate heat. Stir in the vanilla; then cool. Beat the egg yolks with half the sugar until pale and thick. Fold in the cooled chocolate mixture.

In a separate bowl, beat the egg whites until stiff, gradually adding the remaining sugar. Fold the two together. Sift the flour, measure to 3¼ cups, and sift again with the baking powder. Gradually fold into wet ingredients to make a stiff dough. Fold in the nuts.

With lightly floured hands, form the dough into a cylinder about 1½ inches wide and 10 inches long. Place on a lightly greased baking sheet; brush all over with the beaten egg white. Bake for 45 minutes or until the dough is set. Remove from the baking sheet and cut the dough on the diagonal into ½-inch-thick slices.

Toast the biscotti on the baking sheet for 5 to 8 minutes on each side or until slightly dry. Stored in an airtight container, the biscotti will keep for 2 weeks.

Beautiful, ambrosial tangerine sherbet is a refreshing way to bring this rich meal to an end. A great favorite at Loaves and Fishes, the sherbet is a blend of frozen tangerine juice, Grand Marnier, cream and egg whites. It can't fail to please. Let it soften slightly before serving.

OPPOSITE: Tangerine sherbet and chocolate biscotti—the perfect ending to a perfect feast

TANGERINE SHERBET

SERVES 6

1 6-ounce can frozen tangerine juice
Grated rind of 1 orange
1 tablespoon Grand Marnier

½ cup sugar
1 cup whipping cream
2 large egg whites
½ teaspoon cream of tartar

Put the frozen juice, orange rind, Grand Marnier, and sugar in a bowl. Set aside and allow the juice to partially thaw—it should be mushy but still frozen. Stir to dissolve the sugar.

Beat the cream until stiff peaks form. Fold into the juice mixture.

Beat the egg whites with the cream of tartar until stiff. Fold a third of the tangerine-and-cream mixture into the egg whites; then fold the egg whites into the remaining tangerine mixture. Pour the sherbet into a 1-quart container, cover with a tight-fitting lid, and place, upside down, in your freezer for 30 minutes. Turn upright and leave frozen until ready to serve.

Tailgate Picnic

*T*he term *tailgate picnic* conjures visions of an elaborate al fresco luncheon among tweed- and plaid-tailored postgraduates anticipating a big win at the Saturday-afternoon football game in the glow of fall's fine shimmering weather. But the tradition takes many forms: Champagne and caviar for the swells, ham and cheese sandwiches from a brown paper bag for those of simpler tastes.

I have created a tailgaters' menu at once genteel (I hope) but still quite simple, styled for any bucolic occasion that puts your car on the road in this perfect season for outdoor enjoyment—fall foliage viewing, harvest time for fruits like apples and grapes, a football game. Use any excuse that occurs to you, pack up the car with all you need—food in plastic containers, good plates, mugs and cutlery, cushions, folding chairs, the dog, whatever (you have a car to take you right to your destination so there is no need to stint on conveniences and comforts). When you arrive, spread a plaid wool blanket on the ground and feast with your friends in the open air. (If you bring the dog, bring his dog food, too, or he will fatten himself on your calzone.)

ORDER OF PREPARATION

*M*ake the soup and the cookies the day before the picnic. Reheat the soup before departure and keep it steaming hot by pouring it into a wide-necked Thermos rinsed first with boiling water. A tightly capped Thermos will keep the soup hot for at least 6 hours. Start the calzone early in the morning of the picnic and assemble the salad just before take-off.

Do bring along some of your nice things—plates, napkins, etc.—and reserve the plastic for containers carrying the food. Tighten lids to avert disaster. If you are taking a hamper or large picnic basket, remember to pack foods in reverse order: The food you will eat first should go in last. For a different twist, wrap the calzone in clear cellophane and tie with colored pipe cleaners.

Wine suggestion: Serve a lovely medium-bodied Zinfandel, always perfect for a picnic.

ROASTED EGGPLANT AND RED PEPPER SOUP

SERVES 6

2 pounds Japanese eggplants
3 large sweet red peppers
⅛ teaspoon saffron threads
4 cups chicken stock, preferably homemade
3 tablespoons olive oil
2 garlic cloves, peeled and minced
1 large onion, finely chopped
2 medium-size ripe plum tomatoes, peeled and coarsely chopped (or 1 16-ounce canned whole tomatoes)

2 tablespoons freshly squeezed lemon juice
Salt and freshly ground black pepper to taste

GARNISH
¼ cup coarsely chopped fresh coriander
Dollop of sour cream or whipped cream

The charred eggplant and peppers lend this soup a marvelous smoky flavor.

Preheat the broiler. Cover the broiler pan with a sheet of aluminum foil and spread the eggplant and peppers on it. Place them as close to the flame as possible, turning them frequently until they are charred and blistered all over, about 5 minutes on each side.

Put the charred peppers in a plastic or brown paper bag, seal it tightly, and allow to steam for 10 minutes. Scoop out the flesh from the eggplants and discard the skins. Coarsely chop the eggplant flesh. Peel the blackened skins from the red peppers and discard the seeds and stems. Coarsely chop the peppers.

Dissolve the saffron in the chicken stock and bring to a simmer.

Heat the olive oil in a 4-quart saucepan and sauté the garlic and onion over medium heat until translucent. Add the eggplant, peppers, and tomatoes. Stir well. Pour the simmering stock over the vegetables, bring to a simmer, and cook, uncovered, for 15 minutes. Stir in lemon juice.

Purée the soup in several batches in a food processor or blender. Return it to the saucepan and heat until very hot but not simmering. Correct the seasoning with additional salt and pepper. Ladle the hot soup into a heated Thermos and seal. Serve garnished with chopped coriander and bread sticks.

Should you serve this soup at home, garnish with coriander and a dollop of sour or whipped cream.

"When I have carside picnics in Europe and in America, there are good glasses along, good forks and knives, and, if possible, china plates. I would rather smuggle a few dirty plates into my hotel to wash, wherever I happen to be, than eat food on paper plates."
JAMES BEARD
Delights and Prejudices

A glorious tailgate picnic laid out on a trusty car rug—soup, calzone, salad, breadsticks, pecan-date cookies, and autumnal fruits

These individual-size calzone make the perfect picnic companion.

CORNMEAL CALZONE FILLED WITH OLIVES AND CHEESE

SERVES 6

1½ tablespoons active dry
   yeast
⅓ cup lukewarm water
2¼ cups all-purpose flour
¾ cup plus 2 tablespoons
   yellow cornmeal
¾ teaspoon salt
¾ cup lukewarm water
3 tablespoons olive oil
FILLING
   4 tablespoons olive oil
   3 garlic cloves, peeled and
      minced
   1 small onion, finely
      chopped

2 tablespoons chopped fresh
   oregano, or 1 tablespoon
   dried oregano
4 tablespoons chopped fresh
   basil, or 2 tablespoons
   dried basil
¼ cup whole-milk ricotta
   cheese
¼ pound Teleme cheese,
   cubed
¼ cup freshly grated
   Parmesan cheese
4 ounces prosciutto,
   coarsely chopped
¼ cup pitted and coarsely
   chopped olives

In a large mixing bowl, mix together the yeast, ⅓ cup water, and ¼ cup of the flour with a wooden spoon, beating for a few minutes until elastic. Cover with a damp cloth and let it rise in a warm place for 15 to 20 minutes. (The top of the stove over the pilot light is a good spot.)

Then add the remaining flour, ¾ cup of the cornmeal, the salt, lukewarm water, and olive oil. Mix the dough together with a wooden spoon until elastic. Knead for 8 to 10 minutes on a lightly floured board or in an electric mixer fitted with a dough hook. For a light crisp crust add as little additional flour as possible while kneading.

To prevent a crust from forming, rub the mixing bowl with a little olive oil and place the dough back in the bowl. Turn the dough around in the bowl to coat all surfaces with a little oil. Cover with a damp cloth and put it in a warm place to rise for 1 hour.

Make the filling while you wait for the dough to rise. Sauté the garlic and onion in the oil over medium heat until translucent but not brown. Add the oregano and basil and cook for 1 minute more. Cool.

In a bowl, beat the ricotta cheese until smooth. Mix in the Teleme and Parmesan cheese, prosciutto, olives, and cooled onion mixture.

Preheat the oven to 450° to 500° F., or as high as it will go.

For the best crust, bottom and top, heat a pizza stone, unglazed tile, or thin baking sheet in the oven. Punch down the dough and divide it into 6 equal pieces. Roll each piece into an 8-inch circle, ⅛ to ¼ inch thick. Put some of the filling on one half of the dough leaving a 1-inch margin at the edges. Moisten the edges with water and fold the dough over the filling. Fold the edges of the dough onto itself and pinch the edges together to seal.

Sprinkle the heated stone or baking sheet with the remaining 2 tablespoons of cornmeal and slide the calzones onto it. Bake for 18 to 20 minutes or until golden. Remove from the oven and brush the tops with a little olive oil. Cool on a wire rack.

"**The**
trees are in their autumn beauty,
The woodland paths are dry.
Under the October twilight the water
Mirrors a still sky."
W. B. YEATS

FALL SALAD

SERVES 6

DRESSING
- 2 tablespoons light mustard seeds
- 2/3 cup olive oil
- 1/4 cup freshly squeezed lemon juice
- 1 tablespoon mustard
- 1 teaspoon salt
- 1/4 teaspoon sugar

- 2 fennel bulbs
- 1/2 medium-size head red cabbage, shredded
- 1 small head curly endive, washed and torn into bite-size pieces
- 1 green apple, cored and cut into 1/2-inch chunks

Prepare the dressing. Roast the mustard seeds in a heavy skillet over medium heat, stirring constantly, for 1 to 2 minutes or until golden. Be careful not to burn them. Crush in a mortar, leaving some seeds whole.

In a small bowl, whisk together all the remaining dressing ingredients with the crushed seeds until blended thoroughly.

Prepare the salad. Remove the green tops of the fennel and discard them. Cut out the cores and remove any tough outer layers. Cut the bulbs lengthwise into thin strips. Toss with the remaining vegetables and apple in a large bowl. Pour on the dressing and toss well. Cover and refrigerate until ready to pack. The salad should marinate in the dressing for at least 30 minutes.

It is difficult to take a green salad on a picnic because it tends to wilt, and salads with mayonnaise must be kept cold. But no harm will come if the cabbage and fennel soften in this delicious vinaigrette.

PECAN-DATE COOKIES

MAKES TWELVE 3-INCH COOKIES

- 1/2 cup (1 stick) unsalted butter, softened
- 1/4 cup granulated sugar
- 1/4 cup packed dark brown sugar
- 1 large egg, lightly beaten
- 1/2 teaspoon vanilla extract

- 1 cup all-purpose flour
- 1/2 teaspoon baking soda
- 3/4 cup chopped dates
- 2 1/4 ounces pecans, coarsely chopped (1/2 cup plus 1 tablespoon)

Preheat the oven to 375° F.

Cream the butter with the sugars. Add the egg and vanilla extract and beat until smooth.

Combine the flour and baking soda. Gradually add the flour mixture to the wet ingredients and mix well. Stir in the chopped dates and pecans. Drop by rounded tablespoons onto an ungreased baking sheet. Bake for 10 to 12 minutes. Cool on a wire rack and store in an airtight container.

Chewy and satisfying, these are a breeze to make and disappear quickly.

Thyme-marinated roast pork, fried polenta, and lightly cooked Brussels sprouts. Who wouldn't love such riches?

A Passion for Pork

The general disregard for pork is, I think, mainly a matter of provenance—in this case, the pig. We have all been exposed to our share of greasy chops or dry breaded pork medallions with all the subtle flavor of a volleyball. In spite of these experiences and in the face of the growing trend toward less meat in our diet, with the coming of colder weather I crave a little pork, especially a moist, herbed loin of pork served with harvest accompaniments in the crackling glow of fall's first fireplace fire.

Properly prepared, this is a tender meat, delicate of flavor and versatile, that works well in combination with some of my favorite fall foods: fennel, cheese-infused polenta, and Brussels sprouts. By including sprouts in my menu for a roast pork dinner I am selecting a second food about which many of us feel negatively. Sprouts are hated because we overcook them, a skill we no doubt learned from the English. Let's not do it. Sprouts are very good when they are properly cooked and a perfect friend for a roast of pork.

M·e·n·u

PURÉE OF FENNEL SOUP

·

THYME-MARINATED
ROAST PORK

·

FRIED POLENTA

·

BRUSSELS SPROUTS

·

SALAD OF ENDIVE, PEAR,
AND MAYTAG BLUE CHEESE

·

STUFFED DATES
WITH CARAMEL SAUCE

ORDER OF PREPARATION

You can make the soup and cook the polenta a day ahead of the dinner. Start marinating the pork the night before if you wish or early the next morning. Two hours before your guests arrive, begin roasting the pork (and cook the polenta if you

ABOVE: Purée of fennel soup, elegant and flavorful

haven't already done so). Stuff the dates and make the caramel sauce. Prepare the salad greens and vinaigrette and chill the greens in the refrigerator. At the last minute, heat the soup, cook the sprouts, and fry the polenta.

Wine suggestion: Try an earthy, full-bodied Cabernet Sauvignon.

I adore the taste of fennel. As soon as it comes into season I use it as often as I can. This anise-perfumed purée is one of the best fall soups, elegant and packed with flavor. The soup may be made ahead and reheated.

PURÉE OF FENNEL SOUP

SERVES 6

4 large fennel bulbs (about
   1½ pounds), washed and
   trimmed
3 medium-size onions,
   chopped
2 tablespoons olive oil
8 tablespoons (1 stick)
   unsalted butter
1 tablespoon tomato paste

8 cups chicken broth,
   preferably homemade
   Bouquet garni of bay leaf,
   parsley sprigs, and fennel
   sprigs tied in cheesecloth
2 tablespoons all-purpose
   flour
   Salt and freshly ground
   black pepper to taste

Discard the top and tough outer leaves of the fennel, reserving some of the top sprigs for the bouquet garni and to garnish the soup. Cut the bulbs into quarters. Slice the quarters into thin slices.

In a saucepan, sauté the onions in the olive oil and 6 tablespoons of the butter until translucent but not brown. Add the fennel and cook until soft. Add the tomato paste and cook over low heat for 15 to 20 minutes, stirring occasionally. When the vegetables are very tender, purée the mixture in a food processor fitted with a steel blade or through a food mill. Return the purée to the saucepan, add the chicken stock and bouquet garni and simmer, uncovered, for 20 to 30 minutes or until the soup is reduced by a third.

Remove the bouquet garni. Rub the flour and the remaining 2 tablespoons of butter together to form a smooth paste. Stir the beurre manie ½ teaspoon at a time into the hot soup until it is all incorporated and the soup begins to thicken. Season with salt and pepper. Garnish each serving with chopped fennel sprigs.

E very time I make this, I can't believe how delicious it is. No prunes, apricots, or Chinese exoticisms adulterate the final product. A good, homemade tomato sauce enriches the flavor of pan drippings from the cooked roast.

THYME-MARINATED ROAST PORK

SERVES 6

3 garlic cloves, peeled
¼ cup finely chopped fresh
   parsley
1 tablespoon dried thyme
1 tablespoon olive oil
   Salt
1 cup dry white wine
1 5- to 7-pound boneless
   pork loin

Freshly ground black
   pepper to taste
1 small onion, finely
   chopped
2 garlic cloves, peeled and
   finely minced
1 cup tomato sauce,
   preferably homemade
1 tablespoon unsalted butter

In the bowl of a food processor fitted with a steel blade or a blender, process the 3 garlic cloves, parsley, thyme, olive oil, 1 teaspoon of salt, and 1 tablespoon of the wine to a smooth paste.

With a sharp knife, make small slits in the meat. Force generous quantities of the paste into the slits. Rub the remaining mixture all over the roast. Put the pork in a large roasting pan and pour on the remaining wine. Cover and marinate, unrefrigerated, for several hours or refrigerate overnight, turning the meat several times.

Preheat the oven to 400° F.

Drain off and reserve the wine. Sprinkle the top of the roast with salt and pepper and roast for 10 to 15 minutes. Lower the oven temperature to 325° F. and cook for approximately 2 hours more or until a meat thermometer reads 185° F. (approximately 35 minutes per pound). Transfer the roast to a heated serving platter, remove the string, and keep the roast warm.

Pour off all but 2 tablespoons of fat from the roasting pan. Add the onion and remaining garlic and sauté gently for 2 to 3 minutes. Deglaze the pan with the reserved wine over high heat. Add the tomato sauce and cook until reduced to half. Remove from the heat and swirl in the butter. Correct the seasoning with salt and pepper. Carve the roast into thin slices and serve with spoonfuls of the sauce.

"Everything in a pig is good. What ingratitude has permitted his name to become a term of opprobrium."
GRIMOND DE LA REYNIERE

FRIED POLENTA

SERVES 6

4 tablespoons unsalted
   butter
½ onion, finely chopped
4 cups water
1 cup stone-ground yellow
   cornmeal (polenta)

½ teaspoon salt
½ teaspoon finely ground
   black pepper
½ cup heavy cream
¼ pound Gorgonzola cheese,
   crumbled

Polenta, a creamy cornmeal mush the color of a golden harvest moon, has been the staple of Northern Italian cuisine for centuries. A dish that once required an hour or more of stirring can now be prepared quickly thanks to modern cornmeal.

This recipe was given to me by Gary Danko, one of the best new American chefs. A similar recipe was suggested to me by Joan Comendant, assistant chef at Inglenook Winery, who thought it a "pretty simple way to make polenta." She is right.

Preheat the oven to 350° F. Generously butter a shallow 2-quart baking dish. (I like to cut and fry the polenta in rectangles rather than wedges, so I use an 8-inch-square baking pan.)

Melt 2 tablespoons of the butter in a large saucepan. When the foam subsides, add the onions and sauté for 3 to 5 minutes or until soft. Add the water and bring to a boil. Turn the heat to medium-low and slowly add the cornmeal, stirring constantly with a wooden spoon until all the liquid has been absorbed, about 5 minutes. Stir in the salt, pepper, and heavy cream. Remove from the heat and stir in the cheese.

Pour the cornmeal mixture into the prepared pan. Smooth the top with a rubber spatula and bake for 20 minutes or until firm. Cool to room temperature. The polenta may be prepared to this stage up to a day in advance and then covered and refrigerated. Bring to room temperature before frying.

Cut the polenta into 2 × 4-inch rectangles, ½ inch thick. Melt the remaining 2 tablespoons of butter in a large skillet and fry the polenta slices for 2 to 3 minutes on each side or until lightly golden. Drain on paper towels and serve immediately.

Brussels Sprouts

SERVES 6

1½ pounds Brussels sprouts,
    washed and trimmed
2 tablespoons salt

2 to 4 tablespoons unsalted
    butter
Freshly ground black
    pepper

Drop the Brussels sprouts in a large kettle containing several quarts of salted boiling water. Bring to a boil again over high heat and cook for 5 to 8 minutes, depending on the size and age of the sprouts. Drain in a colander and refresh with very cold water; then pat dry.

Melt the butter in a large skillet, add the sprouts and shake them over medium heat for 3 to 5 minutes or until barely golden. Season with additional salt and pepper, if you wish, and serve at once.

This attractive salad has an intriguing combination of flavors. The sharp cheese and peppery watercress cut the sweetness of the pears, leaving a clean palate for dessert. I always use Maytag blue, a delicious blue-veined domestic cheese produced since the 1920s by the same family that makes the equally excellent washing machines.

Salad of Endive, Pear, and Maytag Blue Cheese

SERVES 6

DRESSING
¼ cup red wine or sherry
    vinegar
2 teaspoons Dijon mustard
    Salt to taste
¾ cup walnut or hazelnut
    oil

1 Belgian endive, washed
    and broken into bite-size
    pieces

1 ripe pear, peeled and
    sliced lengthwise
1 small bunch fresh
    watercress
¼ pound Maytag (or any
    good) blue cheese,
    crumbled
¼ cup walnuts, lightly
    toasted and coarsely
    chopped

To make the dressing, combine the vinegar, mustard, and salt in a bowl. Slowly whisk in the oil until thoroughly blended.

In another bowl, toss the endive, pear, and watercress with enough dressing to coat them lightly. Divide among salad plates and top each salad with a little crumbled cheese and a few toasted walnuts.

Julie Wagner is one of the best cooks I know in Napa Valley. She brought this confection back with her from one of her many trips to Italy. Medjools are dark oversize dates, very sweet and moist. Considered the premier date, they can be found in gourmet shops and health food stores.

Stuffed Dates with Caramel Sauce

SERVES 6

¼ pound mascarpone cheese
    Grated rind of 1 lemon

12 pitted Medjool dates at
    room temperature

A delectable morsel: a Medjool date stuffed
with mascarpone cheese on a bed
of caramel sauce with a sprinkling
of grated orange

CARAMEL SAUCE
½ cup sugar
6 tablespoons water
1 tablespoon unsalted butter

2 teaspoons freshly squeezed
  lemon juice
2 teaspoons Cognac
  Grated rind of 1 orange

To prepare the dates, beat the mascarpone until light and fluffy; then add the lemon rind. Fill each date with a rounded tablespoon of the mixture.

To make the caramel sauce, put the sugar in a heavy light-colored saucepan with 2 tablespoons of the water. Let stand until the sugar is moistened. Cook over medium-high heat to a pale golden brown, occasionally moving the pan. Do not stir the sugar mixture and do not allow it to come to a boil. Gradually add the remaining 4 tablespoons of water and cook over medium heat until the sugar is dissolved. Remove from the heat and swirl in the butter, and then the lemon juice and Cognac.

Pour a little caramel sauce onto individual lightly buttered dessert plates. Top with two of the dates and sprinkle with the orange rind. Serve with strong black coffee.

"Almost every person has something secret he likes to eat."
M.F.K. FISHER

A Wild
and Gathered
Dinner

*E*very fall, after the first soaking rains, the forests of North America yield a lavish secret harvest—a profusion of wild mushrooms. For country dwellers enamored of food gathering, this is the time to combine the satisfactions of a good hunt with the pleasures of a long walk in the autumn woods. If success crowns your adventure and you reap a basketful of the prized, trumpet-shaped chanterelles, hurry home with your treasure and make this elegant dinner.

The "supermarket" mushroom (the white, flavorless, cultivated form of the meadow mushroom *Agaricus bisporus*) has had its day; increasingly we are developing a taste for the subtle, earthy flavors of our wild mushrooms. The lustrous butter-flavored chanterelle *(Cantharellus cibarius)* was once imported exclusively from Europe, but it has been here all along—and we are finding it, buried on the rich forest floors of northern New England, Pennsylvania, Michigan, and the Pacific Northwest. Do not eat *any* wild mushroom without first consulting someone well informed on the subject or a reliable guidebook. Fresh chanterelles can also be found in some specialty markets, in season.

When you are fortunate enough to dine on fresh chanterelles, keep the rest of the meal simple; the mushrooms need no elaborate background. Here the bay laurel soup makes a light but invigorating introduction. The risotto is robust and satisfying. And the dessert—a freshly baked nut tart—is far less filling than it sounds. This is a hearty dinner, not a heavy one.

ORDER OF PREPARATION

*A*lthough you must stand at the stove and stir the risotto for 35 minutes, it is the only thing on the menu that demands close attention. On the day before the dinner or in the morning, make the tart. The heating of the stock with the bay leaves can also be done well in advance.

One hour before dinner, boil the potatoes while you toast the croutons. Keep the croutons warm in a low oven. Make the potato purée. Wash the greens and prepare the dressing for the salad. If you are serving cream with the tart, whip it now. Start the risotto 45 minutes before you wish to sit down.

Serve the soup hot with the croutons and purée. Save the bread for the salad and cheese course. The risotto looks innocent, but it is surprisingly rich. Let it stand on its own, and savor the taste. Follow it with the salad and cheese. Serve the nut tart at room temperature.

Wine suggestion: Along with a perfect climate for wild mushrooms, Oregon produces soft, well-rounded Pinot Noir. Try one.

BAY LAUREL SOUP WITH POTATO PURÉE

SERVES 6

8 whole fresh or dried bay
  leaves
2 quarts beef or veal stock,
  preferably homemade or
  high-quality frozen stock
  (see margin note)
4 large egg yolks, beaten

CROUTONS
6 ½-inch-thick slices Italian
  bread, preferably
  homemade
2 to 3 tablespoons unsalted
  butter

Potato Purée (recipe
  follows)

*A*n appetite stimulant, this soup is Provençal in origin and, in this version, derives its intense flavor from the California bay laurel (*Umbellularia california*). If you don't have access to bay trees, use dried bay leaves.

In a large saucepan, simmer the bay leaves in the stock for 20 minutes; then remove and discard the leaves. Stir a little of the hot broth into the beaten egg yolks; then stir the yolks back into the broth and heat but do not allow to boil.

While the soup is simmering, sauté the bread in the butter in a frying pan until the bread is lightly golden on each side. Drain on paper towels.

To serve, ladle the soup into warm bowls. Float a crouton topped with a heaping spoonful of the Potato Purée in each serving. (If you wish, garnish each serving with a fresh bay laurel leaf.)

An unusual topping with an elusive flavor. More than the sum of its parts.

POTATO PURÉE

SERVES 6

2 medium-size potatoes,
   peeled
2 garlic cloves, peeled
1 teaspoon salt, or to taste

¼ cup fruity virgin olive oil
Freshly ground black
   pepper to taste

Put the potatoes in a pot of salted water and bring to a boil. Cook for 20 to 25 minutes or until very soft. Drain the potatoes.

In a food processor purée the garlic and salt into a paste. Add the potatoes and mix until smooth. With the machine running, gradually add up to ¼ cup of olive oil to make a smooth thick paste. Correct the seasoning.

A good risotto should be creamy, firm, and chewy. This takes patience and a lot of stirring. Short-grain Italian rice is essential; it is the only rice that produces a creamy sauce while retaining its shape. The furled, apricot-hued chanterelles sing out against the simple background of the rice.

WILD MUSHROOM RISOTTO

SERVES 6

7 to 8 cups beef broth,
   preferably homemade (see
   Note)
1 pound fresh chanterelles or
   porcini mushrooms, well
   rinsed, dried, and cut into
   ½-inch slices (see Note)
2 to 3 tablespoons unsalted
   butter

4 cups Arborio rice, or any
   short-grain rice (see
   margin note)
¼ cup finely chopped fresh
   Italian parsley (optional)
Salt and freshly ground
   black pepper to taste
¼ cup freshly grated
   Parmesan cheese

Bring the beef broth to a simmer.

In a large heavy-bottomed casserole, sauté the mushrooms in the butter over medium heat for 10 to 15 minutes or until tender. Set aside. Add the rice and turn it several times until it is well coated with the butter. Add ½ cup of the simmering broth. Stir constantly with a wooden spoon to keep the rice from sticking to the pan. When the broth has been completely absorbed, add another ½ cup of broth. Continue cooking over medium heat while stirring all the time, adding a ½ cup of broth at a time as the broth is absorbed, until the rice is tender but still firm (al dente), about 30 to 35 minutes. Add the reserved mushrooms after the risotto has been cooking for 20 minutes. The risotto should have a slight amount of creamy liquid when finished. Taste and correct the seasoning, adding more salt and lots of freshly ground pepper. If you wish, sprinkle with chopped parsley before serving. Serve immediately accompanied with a bowl of freshly grated cheese.

NOTES: An overly salty canned broth ruins the delicate risotto; if you don't have homemade stock, use water or a good store-bought frozen stock.

Although it is advisable to avoid washing mushrooms, I find it impossible to clean chanterelles any other way. Brush as much dirt from the mushrooms as possible; then quickly rinse off any remaining dirt under cold water. Wipe dry immediately with a soft cloth. If you are not using the mushrooms right away, dry them in a 180° F. oven for 10 to 15 minutes with the door open. They will keep for up to a week in the refrigerator.

Freshly gathered chanterelle mushrooms

The delicate risotto is enhanced by a bitter salad, assorted cheeses, and a nut-filled tart.

This salid is a visual delight—a colorful blend of the last bitter greens from the winter garden. Use lots of Italian parsley if you can get it. Just be sure to choose from whatever is the freshest. The hazelnut dressing works as a flavor bridge between the main course and the nut tart.

BITTER FALL SALAD

SERVES 6

DRESSING
1/3 cup sherry vinegar
2 shallots, minced
1 tablespoon Dijon mustard
Salt
3/4 cup hazelnut oil
1/4 cup olive oil

6 cups greens, well washed,
dried, and torn into bite-
size pieces, such as
arugula, mache, curly
endive, red leaf lettuce,
radicchio, romaine lettuce,
spinach, watercress, and
Italian parsley

To make the dressing, combine the vinegar, shallots, mustard, and salt in a bowl. Slowly whisk in the oils until thick.

Toss the salad greens with the dressing until well blended, and serve immediately.

Nuts are at their freshest now. This tart, reminiscent of a classic pecan pie but nowhere near as gooey and sweet, affords a fine opportunity to sample the harvest.

NUTTY TART

SERVES 6

SWEET PASTRY DOUGH
3 tablespoons unsalted
butter, softened
7/8 cup all-purpose flour
4 tablespoons sugar
1/8 teaspoon salt
2 large egg yolks, beaten
1 to 2 tablespoons ice water
FILLING
1½ cups whole unsalted
nuts, such as walnuts,
filberts, pecans, almonds,
Brazil nuts, macadamia
nuts, or peanuts

2 large eggs, beaten
1/4 cup packed light brown
sugar
1/4 cup honey
2 tablespoons unsalted
butter, melted
1/2 teaspoon grated orange
rind
1/2 teaspoon brandy or
Grand Marnier
GARNISH
Lightly beaten whipping
cream

First prepare the pastry. In a mixing bowl, cut the butter into the flour, sugar, and salt with a pastry blender until it resembles coarse meal. Add the egg yolks, one at a time, thinning each time with a little of the water. Work the mixture until sufficiently blended. Gather into a ball, knead twice, and flatten with the palm of your hand. Wrap the pastry in plastic wrap and refrigerate for at least 30 minutes before using.

Preheat the oven to 350° F. Spread the nuts on a baking sheet and lightly toast them for 5 to 8 minutes. Cool.

Press the pastry dough into an 8-inch tart pan with a removable rim. Chill for 30 minutes.

Preheat the oven to 350° F. Prepare the filling. Combine the eggs, brown sugar, honey, butter, orange rind, and brandy and mix well. Stir in the nuts. Pour the mixture into the chilled tart shell and bake for 30 to 35 minutes. Let cool and remove the pan rim. Serve small slices with a dollop of whipped cream.

Fair Game

*H*untsmen bearing fresh furred and feathered trophies to our door are infrequent visitors for most of us these days, and it is only the occasional country freezer that is stockpiled for winter with the local bounty of field and forest. Be that as it may, a hearty game dinner—glorious food that is uniquely autumnal—should be shared between friends at least once every year in the fall season.

I offer this menu starring the common rabbit. Favored more in France than in this country, where it has a way of being consigned to spiritless stews, rabbit is delectable fare, with a light gamy taste of the wild. It has the lean flesh of most game, is very low in fat, and has a mild flavor reminiscent of the dark meat of a good free-range chicken. Today it can be found (often frozen) in many supermarkets or at your butcher's and it is generally inexpensive. Marinating the rabbit overnight and grilling it with frequent bastings produces a tender result and obviates the whole business of hanging the animal if it has come to you fresh from the field. (Wild rabbit has a more pronounced "gamy" flavor than the domestic rabbit and should be eaten when it is young.)

Two things are good companions for rabbit: black beans and Beaujolais. I learned about the affinity of rabbit and beans when I enjoyed this excellent combination at Mustard's Grill in Napa Valley. The first Beaujolais of the year usually reaches our shores about the time the hunting season opens and the fruitiness of the wine is a fine complement to the rabbit. Celebrate the fresh game and new wine together.

M·e·n·u

MAUI ONION RINGS
WITH SAGE LEAVES
·
BROILED RABBIT HUNTER STYLE
·
BLACK BEANS WITH PECANS
·
SALSA CRUDA
·
STEAMED KALE
WITH BALSAMIC BUTTER
·
SKILLET CORN BREAD
·
APPLE TART

ABOVE: *A succulent serving of Maui onion rings with sage leaves*

OPPOSITE: *Broiled rabbit served with black beans with pecans and salsa cruda, an inspired combination*

ORDER OF PREPARATION

*T*his menu may, at first glance, appear to entail a lot of labor, but once the apple tart is done, the preparation of the remaining dishes is really very simple. The night before marinate the rabbit, soak the beans, and make the apple tart crust.

To prepare for dinner, cook the beans and complete the tart begun the night before. Next, make the salsa, cut up and soak the onions with the sage leaves, and prepare the sauce for the beans. Make the corn bread and cook the kale at the last minute. Cook the onion rings as the guests arrive. Broil the rabbit. Garnish the beans with salsa cruda, sour cream, and fresh coriander and serve on a warm plate. Serve the corn bread straight from the cast-iron skillet. The tart is at its best served warm with crème fraîche, or ice cream and strong black coffee.

Wine suggestion: Serve a slightly chilled French Beaujolais Nouveau.

*H*erbs stimulate the appetite, so why not start the evening with an hors d'oeuvre of an old favorite temptingly flavored with sage?

MAUI ONION RINGS WITH SAGE LEAVES

SERVES 6

1 cup buttermilk
1 cup water
6 Maui, Walla Walla, Vidalia, or sweet yellow onions, peeled and cut into ¼-inch-thick slices
1 cup whole fresh sage leaves

2 cups all-purpose flour
1 tablespoon dried sage leaves
Salt
½ teaspoon freshly ground black pepper
1 24-ounce bottle peanut oil

Combine the buttermilk and water in a bowl and add the onion slices and fresh sage leaves. Let stand in the mixture for 30 minutes. Drain the onions and sage leaves on paper towels. In a brown paper bag, combine the flour, dried sage leaves, 1 teaspoon of salt, and pepper. Dredge the onions and sage leaves in the flour. Heat the oil to 360° F. in a deep-fat fryer or wok. Add the onions and sage leaves to the hot oil and cook until the onion rings rise to the top of the oil. (The sage leaves will cook more quickly than the onion rings, so watch them carefully.) Drain on paper towels and sprinkle with more salt. Serve immediately.

*H*unter style" refers to the time-honored hunters' practice of marinating game overnight in a combination of red wine, olive oil, and juniper berries before cooking it quickly.

BROILED RABBIT HUNTER STYLE

SERVES 6

½ bottle Beaujolais
¼ cup red wine vinegar
½ cup olive oil
1 small onion, sliced
4 unpeeled garlic cloves, halved
1 teaspoon juniper berries, lightly crushed
1 teaspoon dried oregano

1 teaspoon dried thyme
1 teaspoon cracked black pepper
2 bay leaves
1 2- to 2½-pound rabbit, cut into quarters

GARNISH
6 small sprigs fresh thyme (optional)

In a shallow dish large enough to hold the rabbit in one layer, mix the first 10 ingredients together. Toss the rabbit pieces in the marinade and keep covered in a cool place overnight or for at least 12 hours, turning several times.

To broil the rabbit, preheat the broiler. Put the rabbit pieces on a broiler tray and brush liberally with the marinade. Broil for 8 to 10 minutes on each side, brushing frequently with more marinade. The rabbit is done when the meat feels springy but firm to the touch. Garnish each serving with a sprig of thyme.

BLACK BEANS WITH PECANS

SERVES 6

2 cups dried black beans,
   sorted and rinsed
1 onion, peeled and studded
   with 3 whole cloves
½ cup pecan halves
DRESSING
2 medium-size garlic cloves,
   peeled
½ cup olive oil

½ cup bean cooking liquid
3 tablespoons red wine
   vinegar
¼ teaspoon ground allspice
Salt and freshly ground
   black pepper to taste
GARNISH
   Sour Cream
   Chopped fresh corriander

Put the beans in a heavy kettle and cover with 2 quarts of water. Soak overnight.

Add the onion studded with the cloves and cook, uncovered, over medium heat for 1 to 1¼ hours or until the beans are tender but not mushy. Stir occasionally. Drain the beans, reserving ½ cup of the cooking liquid.

Lightly toast the pecans in a hot oven for a few minutes and then coarsely chop them. Add the nuts to the drained beans.

In a small bowl, whisk together the dressing ingredients until they are thoroughly blended. Toss with the warm beans and nuts and taste for seasoning. Garnish each portion with sour cream and coriander.

SALSA CRUDA

MAKES 1½ CUPS

1 ripe tomato, coarsely
   chopped
½ medium-size onion,
   chopped
2 medium-size garlic cloves,
   peeled and chopped

1 to 2 serrano chiles, finely
   chopped
2 tablespoons freshly
   squeezed lemon juce
½ teaspoon salt

Combine all the ingredients in a bowl and mix well. Cover and refrigerate until ready to use. It will keep for 2 to 3 days in the refrigerator.

An excellent companion for a variety of dishes, this spicy condiment is especially delicious with the grilled rabbit and black beans. Since serrano chiles are hot, use more or less depending on your taste. Wear rubber gloves when handling chiles and wash the knife and cutting surface with soapy water immediately after chopping.

The favorite autumn dessert: apple tart

The old Southern tradition of adding a dash of vinegar to the kale heightens the flavor.

STEAMED KALE WITH BALSAMIC BUTTER

SERVES 6

1½ pounds kale, cleaned,
tough stems removed,
and coarsely chopped
2 garlic cloves, peeled and
minced
4 tablespoons balsamic
vinegar

2 tablespoons dry red wine
6 tablespoons unsalted
butter
Salt and freshly ground
black pepper to taste

Steam the kale for 5 to 6 minutes or until just wilted. (The cooking time will vary according to the age and toughness of the greens.)

Put the garlic, vinegar, and red wine into a saucepan and reduce by half over high heat. Remove from the heat and whisk in the butter, 1 tablespoon at a time, until all is incorporated. Season with salt and pepper. Put the kale into a warm serving bowl and spoon the sauce over it.

Skillet-baking the corn bread gives it a nice brown crust.

SKILLET CORN BREAD

SERVES 6

1 cup yellow cornmeal
1 cup all-purpose flour
1 tablespoon baking powder
2 tablespoons sugar

4 scallions, minced
1 egg, lightly beaten
1 cup buttermilk
⅓ cup unsalted butter

Preheat the oven to 400° F. Place an 8-inch cast-iron skillet into the oven to heat for 8 to 10 minutes.

Combine the cornmeal, flour, baking powder, and sugar and mix well. Add the scallions and coat with dry ingredients. Beat the egg and buttermilk together. Remove the frying pan from the oven and melt the butter in the hot pan. Do not let it burn. Add the egg-buttermilk mixture and the melted butter to the dry ingredients and mix until just blended. Pour into hot skillet and bake for 20 to 25 minutes or until golden. Serve right from the skillet or run a knife around the edge and unmold the corn bread onto a wooden board or plate.

THE STAINLESS STEEL (CUISINART), anodized aluminum (Calphalon), and nonstick (Teflon, Silverstone) cookware we have taken to our hearts is all well and good, but there is something to be said for cooking with good old black cast-iron pans: Research tells us (1) a lot of us suffer from iron deficiency and (2) the little bit of iron that is released from the cast iron in cooking is good for us.

APPLE TART

SERVES 6

PASTRY
* 1 cup all-purpose flour
* 1 tablespoon sugar
* 8 tablespoons unsalted butter, cut into 8 pieces
* 2 to 3 tablespoons ice water

FILLING
* 1½ pounds apples, such as Rome, McIntosh, or Jonathan, peeled, cored, and finely chopped
* ¼ cup Calvados or Applejack brandy
* ⅔ cup sugar
* 3 large egg yolks
* 1 cup heavy cream

TOPPING
* 4 tablespoons finely chopped almonds
* ¼ cup packed dark brown sugar
* ¼ cup all-purpose flour
* 2 tablespoons unsalted butter

Simple and sublime, this tart features brandy-soaked apples on a rich crust. You will need an 8-inch tart pan with a removable rim.

To prepare the pastry, combine the flour and sugar in a bowl. Cut the butter into the flour mixture with a pastry cutter or two knives until it resembles coarse meal. Add the ice water a little at a time, quickly stirring the mixture into a rough ball. Gather the dough into a ball and flatten slightly with the palm of your hand. Wrap the dough in plastic wrap and chill for at least 1 hour.

Allow the dough to stand at room temperature until it is malleable. Roll out on a lightly floured surface to a thickness of ⅛ inch. Fold the dough over the rolling pin. Center over the tart pan and unfold. Gently press the dough into the pan so that the edges of the dough extend approximately ⅛ inch higher than the rim of the pan. Prick all over with a fork, cover with plastic wrap, and chill for at least 1 hour before baking (see Note).

Soak the apples for the filling in the calvados for 30 minutes.

Preheat the oven to 425° F.

Bake the chilled crust for 15 minutes. Remove from the oven. Lower the oven temperature to 350° F. Sprinkle the warm crust with 2 tablespoons of the sugar and set aside. Place the tart pan on a baking sheet (to catch drips). Drain the apple slices, reserving the brandy. Heap the apples into the crust and bake for 30 minutes or until soft. Remove from the oven.

Raise the oven temperature to 425° F.

Beat together the reserved brandy, remaining sugar, egg yolks, and cream. Pour over the cooked apples.

Make the topping by combining the chopped almonds, brown sugar, and flour. Work in the butter until the mixture is crumbly. Scatter it evenly over the top of the apples. Return to the oven and bake for 20 to 30 minutes more.

Serve the tart warm or at room temperature accompanied by vanilla ice cream, crème fraîche or whipped cream flavored with a little applejack or calvados.

NOTE: The tart crust may be made several days in advance and then refrigerated or frozen. Defrost before using.

"'Well,'
said Pooh, 'What I like best—' and then he had to stop and think. Because although Eating Honey *was* a very good thing to do, there was a moment just before you began to eat it which was better than when you were, but he didn't know what it was called."

A. A. MILNE
The House at Pooh Corner

Easy Does It

Who among us has lived unacquainted with holiday stress? Or holiday jitters or holiday doldrums or plain old holiday overload. Quite often, it seems to me, it is in the kitchen—bursting with unpacked grocery bags, intrepid cross traffic, and frantic cooking activity—that we feel most of all that we may really go under. To ease the general strain, I suggest this elegant pre-Thanksgiving dinner, which will leave you neither too exhausted nor stuffed to enjoy the full-fledged feast the next day. Because most of us already know what we want to eat at Thanksgiving, and turn time and again to favorite family recipes, I have concentrated instead on composing an easy meal for you to set before early-arriving guests or any and all visiting firemen· who may have collected in your home for the holiday. The bravura bass en papillote looks impressive but really requires little work (just assemble it in the morning, refrigerate, and pop in the oven minutes before serving), and the whole dinner should take little more than an hour of your time, thus leaving you with time and energy to go all out on preparations for the next day.

The principle of light eating is at the heart of the menu. I know of two schools of thought on the best way to conduct oneself before a major feast: Some enthusiastic eaters actually believe it is only right to eat larger and larger meals before a feast, thereby stretching the stomach to a maximum state of preparedness; others think it appropriate to eat lightly the day before so as to arrive at the feast table with a good appetite and a clear conscience. I am opting here for this sensible latter course.

M·e·n·u

SEASONAL VEGETABLES
WITH ROQUEFORT-YOGURT DIP

·

SEA BASS PROVENÇAL
EN PAPILLOTE

·

WILD RICE SALAD

·

ANJOU PEARS
IN LATE-HARVEST RIESLING

·

ASSORTED COOKIES

OPPOSITE: Sea bass Provençal in papillote

My keep-it-simple dinner features highly nutritious, low-calorie dishes, lavishly seasoned with herbs and spices. It is, however, not an austerity meal. The main course, particularly, offers visual and sensory enjoyment, as wafts of fragrant steam escape from moist bass tucked into toasty brown papillotes. Let each guest cut into his own papillote to best savor the aroma.

A cautionary word: If cooking en papillote is new to you and the thought of it causes a tremor of anxiety, this is not the moment to attempt it. Absence of stress is our objective on this occasion, so try the fish at another time when you don't have so much on your mind.

ORDER OF PREPARATION

*I*f you like, poach the pears, make the yogurt dip, and prepare the papillotes in the morning. Refrigerate. An hour before dinner, chop the vegetables, keeping them in ice water in the refrigerator until serving time. Cook the rice and then complete the wild rice salad. The bass takes about 10 to 15 minutes to cook, so put it in the oven just before you are ready to eat. Now have a glass of wine or a spritzer. It won't overwhelm the calorie count and it will relax you.

Wine suggestions: A Chardonnay with good acidity is perfect with the fish. Try a late-harvest Johannisberg Riesling with the pears.

SEASONAL VEGETABLES WITH ROQUEFORT-YOGURT DIP

MAKES ABOUT 1 CUP

Various seasonal vegetables (see suggestions below)

DIP
½ cup lowfat plain yogurt
⅔ cups Roquefort cheese

Wash and trim: radishes, mushrooms, cherry tomatoes, endive, snow peas, green, red, yellow peppers, celery, scallions, fennel, sun chokes, and baby yellow and green zucchini with blossoms attached.

Barely steam or blanch to bring out flavor: cauliflower florets, broccoli florets, carrots, green beans, and Brussels sprouts.

To make the Roquefort-Yogurt Dip, purée the yogurt and the Roquefort cheese in a food processor or blender. Cover and chill until ready to serve.

*S*elect from the multitude of fresh low-calorie fall vegetables in your market. Prepare the vegetables as close to serving time as possible to preserve their flavor and nutrients. The heyday of the grandiose crudité arrangement is past. A simple, attractive display is fine.

SEA BASS PROVENÇAL EN PAPILLOTE

SERVES 6

½ cup dry white wine
⅛ teaspoon saffron threads
  (about 12 strands)
1 teaspoon freshly squeezed
  lemon juice
1 tablespoon unsalted butter
1 garlic clove, peeled and
  minced
6 4- to 6-ounce sea bass
  fillets, or any firm white
  fish, such as red snapper,
  halibut, or tilefish
12 medium-size shrimp,
  shelled and deveined with
  tails left on

1 medium-size carrot,
  peeled and cut into
  julienned strips
1 medium-size zucchini, cut
  in half lengthwise and
  then cut into ¼-inch-thick
  half rounds
12 small mushrooms, cleaned
  and sliced
2 medium-size ripe
  tomatoes, cut in half,
  seeded, and then cut into
  thin strips
6 thyme sprigs
6 fennel sprigs (optional)

This aromatic dish uses the traditional seasonings of Provence—garlic, saffron, and tomatoes. By steaming the fish en papillote and trapping the natural juices, you can stint on heavy amounts of olive oil or butter, thus saving hundreds of calories without compromising taste or texture.

Parchment paper is available in gourmet, grocery, and some hardware stores by the roll or sheet.

In a small saucepan, bring the wine to a simmer. Crumble the saffron threads and add them to the saucepan; simmer for 2 to 3 minutes. Stir in the lemon juice, butter, and garlic. Remove from the heat and keep warm.

Cut out 6 circles of parchment paper much larger than the fish fillets—about 16 inches in diameter. Brush with melted butter on one side of each circle. Arrange a fish fillet, 2 shrimp, and some of the vegetables on top of the fish on the buttered side of the circle. Pour about 1 tablespoon of the warm wine broth over the fish and place a sprig of thyme and a sprig of fennel on top.

Fold the paper over to enclose the fish and vegetables. Start folding and twisting the edge of the papillote to make a pleated edge all around. Insert a straw into the open end (or blow into it) to fill with air. The air space allows moisture to rise and fall back on the fish, making it very moist. Quickly remove the straw and twist the end of the paper tightly closed. Place the papillotes side by side on baking sheets. (The packets can be prepared in the morning and refrigerated until you are ready to bake them. If they collapse, undo one end, inflate again, and reseal before baking.)

Preheat the oven to 500° F. Bake the fish for 8 to 10 minutes, depending on their thickness. Present the fish immediately en papillote, or the packets will wrinkle and deflate. With kitchen scissors or a sharp knife have each guest cut a cross in the top of the packet and tear back the paper. Be sure to enjoy the captured aroma of the fish as it escapes from its envelope.

Because of the walnut oil, this salad has a pronounced nutty flavor which blends richly with the fish.

WILD RICE SALAD

SERVES 6

3 cups wild rice
1 garlic clove, peeled
6 ounces mushrooms, finely chopped
1 bunch scallions, finely chopped
3 tablespoons minced fresh parsley
½ large sweet green pepper, finely chopped

VINAIGRETTE
2 tablespoons walnut oil
2 tablespoons raspberry or red wine vinegar
2 tablespoons water
Juice of ½ lemon
2 tablespoons minced shallots
Salt and freshly ground black pepper to taste

Wash the rice thoroughly under cold running water. Put the rice in a medium-size saucepan, cover with 2 quarts of cold water, and add the garlic. Bring to a boil, lower the heat, and simmer, uncovered, for 15 to 20 minutes or until the grains are just tender. Do not let the rice "pop" open. Drain and cool. Discard the garlic clove.

While the rice is cooling, combine all the ingredients for the vinaigrette in a bowl and whisk together until well blended.

Toss the vegetables and rice together in a serving bowl. Pour on the vinaigrette, toss gently, and season with salt and pepper.

The Riesling lends a sweet taste to the pears without adding a lot of calories.

ANJOU PEARS IN LATE-HARVEST RIESLING

SERVES 6

3 to 4 Anjou pears
Juice of 1 lemon
1 bottle late-harvest Riesling
1½ cups water
3 to 4 whole cinnamon sticks

2 whole star anise
½ teaspoon whole cloves
1 teaspoon whole black or white peppercorns
½ cup freshly squeezed orange juice
Grated rind of 1 orange

Peel the pears, leaving the stems attached. Cut in half and remove the cores. Place the pears in a mixing bowl filled with the water and the lemon juice to prevent discoloration.

Combine the remaining ingredients in a large noncorrodible saucepan and bring to a simmer. Add the pears; they should be barely covered with the liquid, so add more water if necessary. Simmer, uncovered, for 8 to 10 minutes or until the pears can be easily pierced with a knife. Remove from the heat and let the pears cool in the syrup; then cover and chill until serving time.

Serve the pears with some of their syrup and an assortment of good store-bought cookies.

*Poached Anjou pears
served with their syrup*

Home Cooking

I am Southern by birth, and this dinner of home-cooked greens is one of the good things I ate in my childhood. I loved it then and I love it now, so I must be a patriot. The names on the menu conjure the heart and soul of down-home Southern cooking: a "mess" of pungent greens and cornmeal dumplings, benne (the African word for sesame) straws, black-eyed peas, persimmon pudding made from the native American tree of the cotton belt, which is also known as the "Virginia date." It's a rare individual, these days, who doesn't know that this kind of food is invading the menus of chic uptown restaurants across the country. American food is hot, but, hot or not, this is an autumn dinner I would have included in any year for its many country virtues: It's relatively inexpensive, uncommonly nutritious, very comforting, and awfully good. Just remember, as old-fashioned as it may be in spirit, it requires above all the one thing most worshipped by the new cuisine—fresh ingredients cooked with care.

This meal with its centerpiece of smoky ham butt and assertive greens is hefty, elbows-on-the-table fare, and it packs a real wallop. For this reason it is most welcome on weekend nights when your friends have expended some energy at strenuous outdoor activity rather than idled all day at a desk.

ORDER OF PREPARATION

*T*here is a lot of cooking in this menu, so either do some of it ahead or juggle several things at once near dinnertime.

You can assemble the benne seed straws up to several days in advance and keep them frozen. Bake them directly from the freezer moments before your guests arrive. The dessert pudding is not difficult but the custard sauce does require constant attention. It must be stirred steadily while it cooks to keep the eggs from curdling. Make both in advance and keep the pudding at room temperature and the custard sauce chilled. You can either soak the beans overnight or follow the quick-cooking method described on the back of the package.

An hour or so before dinner, cook the beans and toss with the vinaigrette. While the beans are cooking, wash the greens and assemble the casserole. Put it on to simmer 20 minutes before the guests arrive. Make the stewed tomatoes. Have the ingredients ready but do not mix up the dumplings until the last minute. They take about 20 minutes to cook. To achieve light, fluffy dumplings, it is important that you *simmer* and not *boil* them in the broth, and don't remove the cover to peek. If you do, the dumplings will boil rather than steam and drop, at dinnertime, like dead weights to the bottom of the stomach.

Serve dessert at room temperature.

Wine suggestion: Drink beer, wine, or cider with this meal, but don't serve your best wine; the pungent greens will simply overpower it.

BENNE SEED STRAWS

MAKES ABOUT 36 STRAWS

1 pound puff pastry, thawed (available in the frozen food section of good grocery stores)
2 tablespoons Dijon mustard
1 large egg, beaten
⅛ pound Parmesan cheese, freshly grated
⅛ pound Cheddar cheese, freshly grated
½ cup benne seeds (sesame seeds)

On a lightly floured surface roll 1 sheet of the puff pastry into a 12 × 16-inch rectangle. Transfer to a large wax paper–lined baking sheet. Brush the pastry with 1 tablespoon of the mustard and then with half the beaten egg. Sprinkle liberally with the cheese. Roll the remaining sheet of pastry to the same size rectangle and lay it on top. Brush with the remaining mustard and egg. Sprinkle on the benne seeds, cover with wax paper, and refrigerate for 30 minutes. With a very sharp knife trim all sides of the pastry to make them neat and even. Cut the pastry into ⅓ × 16-inch strips (approximately 36 strips). Periodically dip the knife into a little flour to prevent the dough from being pulled or torn. Return to the refrigerator to chill for at least 30 minutes.

Preheat the oven to 400° F.

Tightly twist each strip, pinching the ends to seal. Lay the twists on an ungreased baking sheet, 2 inches apart, and bake for 12 to 15 minutes or until golden. Keep any unbaked twists refrigerated. Wipe the baking sheet dry after each batch to keep the butter that oozes from the pastry from burning.

The straws may be assembled in advance and frozen. Bake directly from the freezer.

*E*asy access to ready-made frozen puff pastry brings this savory hors d'oeuvre within the reach of everyone. Benne, or sesame, seed was brought over from Africa by the slaves.

"I never see any home cooking. All I get is fancy stuff."
PRINCE PHILIP, DUKE OF EDINBURGH

Home cooking updated: down-home greens with cornmeal dumplings, stewed tomatoes, and three-bean vinaigrette

DOWN-HOME GREENS WITH CORNMEAL DUMPLINGS

SERVES 6

4 pounds turnip greens,
  collard greens, mustard
  greens, or kale with coarse
  stems removed, washed
  and coarsely chopped
1 pound pork shoulder butt
  (Have the butcher cut the
  meat to the bone in
  several places)

DUMPLINGS
  ¾ cup cornmeal
  ½ cup all-purpose flour
  1 teaspoon baking powder
  1 tablespoon sugar
  ¼ teaspoon salt
  ¼ cup finely chopped
    scallions
  ½ cup grated Monterey Jack
    cheese
  1 large egg, beaten

In a large noncorrodible casserole, combine the greens with just enough water to cover; then add the pork butt. Bring to a boil, lower heat, and simmer, partially covered, for 25 to 30 minutes or until greens are soft. Uncover and bring to a boil to reduce the liquid by one-third.

Prepare the dumplings in a medium-size mixing bowl. Combine the cornmeal, flour, baking powder, sugar, salt, scallions, and cheese. Make a well in the center and add the beaten egg and ½ cup of broth from the cooked greens. Mix just enough to blend.

Drop heaping tablespoons of the batter onto the simmering greens. Keep the dumplings several inches apart. Cover and continue simmering over moderate heat for 10 to 12 minutes. Uncover and cook for 3 to 5 minutes more or until the dumplings are dry on the top.

Serve with a little hot pepper, vinegar, or Tabasco sauce.

STEWED TOMATOES

SERVES 6

2 tablespoons unsalted
  butter
2 tablespoons olive oil
1 small onion, finely
  chopped
1 small sweet green pepper,
  cored, seeded, and finely
  chopped

4 cups drained canned or
  fresh blanched and peeled
  plum tomatoes
¼ cup whole basil leaves
1 tablespoon freshly
  squeezed lemon juice
  Salt and freshly ground
  black pepper to taste

In a large saucepan, heat the butter and oil. Add the onion and green pepper. Sauté over medium heat until soft. Add the tomatoes, basil, lemon juice, and salt and pepper to taste. Simmer for 8 to 10 minutes or until the tomatoes are heated through.

*P*eerless comfort food—and a wonderful casual dinner requiring little work. Down-home greens are at their very best in the fall, fresh from the garden after the first cold snap. When the delicate lettuces of summer have vanished, the hardy "greens" still stand, lush in color, loaded with important vitamins and minerals. This is an updated, more richly flavored version of the original. The cornmeal dumplings are my addition.

*Serve the benne seed straws
in a homey crock*

THREE-BEAN VINAIGRETTE

SERVES 6

1 cup dried black-eyed peas, sorted and rinsed
1 cup dried cranberry beans, sorted and rinsed
1 cup dried great northern beans, sorted and rinsed
1 onion, peeled and studded with 3 whole cloves
1 cup finely chopped scallions
¼ cup finely chopped fresh Italian parsley

Salt and freshly ground black pepper to taste

VINAIGRETTE
2 garlic cloves, peeled
1 teaspoon salt
1 teaspoon dried rosemary
½ cup olive oil
¼ cup red wine vinegar
Salt and freshly ground black pepper to taste

Cover the beans with cold water and soak overnight. The following day, drain the beans and put them in a saucepan with enough fresh cold water to cover by 2 inches. Add the onion studded with the cloves and bring to a boil. Lower the heat to a simmer and cook, uncovered, for 45 minutes to 1 hour or until the beans are just tender. Drain and reserve ½ cup of the cooking liquid.

In a medium-size bowl prepare the vinaigrette. Mash the garlic, salt, and rosemary to a paste. Whisk in the reserved bean liquid and the vinegar until blended. Slowly add the olive oil until thoroughly incorporated.

Put the warm beans, scallions, and parsley into a salad bowl. Toss thoroughly with the vinaigrette, adding more salt and pepper to taste. Serve warm or at room temperature.

This dessert, so easy to make, is the best way I know to end a down-home dinner. Cinnamon and ginger enhance the tart flavor of the persimmons, and the pudding looks beautiful on the plate surrounded by the custard sauce.

PERSIMMON PUDDING WITH CUSTARD SAUCE

SERVES 6

1 cup golden raisins
½ cup brandy
2 cups persimmon pulp (see Note)
2 large eggs, beaten
½ cup sugar
¼ cup honey
1½ cups all-purpose flour
1 teaspoon baking powder
1 teaspoon baking soda
¼ teaspoon salt

1 teaspoon ground cinnamon
½ teaspoon ground ginger
1 cup milk
½ cup heavy cream
¼ cup (½ stick) unsalted butter, melted
¾ cup coarsely chopped walnuts
Custard Sauce (recipe follows)

Preheat the oven to 350° F. Butter a 10-inch springform pan and line the bottom with wax paper. Soak the raisins in the brandy.

In a large mixing bowl, combine the persimmon pulp, eggs, sugar, and honey until well blended. In a separate bowl, mix together the flour, baking powder, baking soda, salt, cinnamon, and ginger. Stir the dry ingredients alternately with the milk and heavy cream into the persimmon mixture. Add the melted butter and mix well.

Let the batter stand for 10 minutes to thicken. Fold in the brandy-soaked raisins and the nuts. Pour into the prepared pan and bake for 1 hour to 1 hour and 15 minutes or until the pudding is set. Run a knife around the rim and remove while pan is still warm.

Serve warm or at room temperature with the Custard Sauce.

NOTE: Scoop the pulp from the skin of 3 to 4 large persimmons and discard any seeds. Purée the pulp in a blender or food processor.

CUSTARD SAUCE

MAKES 2 CUPS

6 large egg yolks
⅔ cup sugar

2½ cups milk
2 tablespoons brandy

In a large mixing bowl, beat the egg yolks with half the sugar until pale and thick. Combine the milk and remaining sugar in a medium-size saucepan. Stir to dissolve the sugar and bring to a boil. Remove from the heat and gradually whisk the milk mixture into the egg yolk mixture.

Return to the saucepan and cook over low heat, stirring constantly with a wooden spoon and getting into all edges of the pan, for 8 to 10 minutes or until the custard is thick enough to coat the spoon. Do not let the custard simmer or boil. Remove from the heat and stir in the brandy. Serve warm or at room temperature. If you make this ahead of time, cover and refrigerate it until ready to serve. Reheat very slowly in a saucepan over low heat.

"It is hard to judge if one's own mother was a good cook. Hers is the first food we eat and there is nothing to compare it to, and there is so much love around it."

FEDERICO FELLINI

WINTER

The New Meat and Potatoes

M·e·n·u

ROAST
YOUNG SADDLE OF VENISON
WITH CURRANT SAUCE
·
POTATOES AU GRATIN
·
SAUTÉED WATERCRESS
·
GREEN SALAD
·
BRANDIED ORANGES
WITH BURNT SUGAR
AND ALMONDS

*M*eat and potatoes often mean a standing roast of red meat surrounded by billowing mounds of mashed potatoes, once the traditional Sunday dinner in many families. It is very unfashionable now (too much meat, too much cholesterol, too macho, too heavy), but really very, very good. Meat in this country has historically been of remarkable quality, and roasts—haunches, saddles, loins—are a peculiarly American glory. They can be prepared in a way that is new and perfectly healthy.

The hunters' prize of venison, oddly overlooked in our era, was more plentiful than domestic fowl or pigs in early settlement days. It had a brief vogue as a luxury dish in the mid-nineteenth century, but it is only recently that it has enjoyed renewed popularity. Raised commercially in New Zealand and exported, venison reaches us, often frozen, in an "ungamy" condition, for unlike wild deer the diet of the animals has been controlled. The meat, aged like beef, is lean, tender, and moist and needs no marinating except for the purpose of imparting flavor. What's more, the saddle is a very easy cut to roast. The au gratin potatoes are a perfect accompaniment, but, while you may have been hearing that potatoes are really *not* fattening—well, these *are*.

ORDER OF PREPARATION

*T*he focus of this meal is the venison, so I have done away with the first course; I don't think all those Sunday rib roast dinners began with anything but ravenous appetites. If you want to be really American, you can be so bold as to serve the salad first. The timing for this meal is not temperamental and all the cooking is comparatively easy. Remember to begin marinating the roast the night before; then just decide when you want to sit down to dinner, back up about 2 hours, and start there.

Begin to roast the venison while you prepare the potatoes. Lower the oven temperature and bake the potatoes in the same oven while the roast finishes cooking. Peel the oranges and marinate, carmelize the sugar and whip the cream. Wash the greens and make the salad dressing. Just before you carve the roast, sauté the watercress and make the currant sauce. Assemble dessert just before serving. The brandied oranges make a light, satisfying finish to the dinner.

Wine suggestion: This elegant and moderately expensive meal deserves an equally memorable wine. Splurge on a sturdy full-bodied Cabernet Sauvignon.

ROAST YOUNG SADDLE OF VENISON WITH CURRANT SAUCE

SERVES 6

MARINADE
- ½ cup olive oil
- 1 bottle dry white wine
- 2 carrots, peeled and coarsely chopped
- 1 medium-size onion, thinly sliced
- 2 celery stalks with leaves, coarsely chopped
- 3 garlic cloves, mashed and peeled
- 1 fresh or dried bay leaf
- 1 teaspoon crushed juniper berries
- Several parsley sprigs
- 1 thyme sprig
- ⅛ teaspoon whole cloves

- 1 3½- to 4-pound saddle of venison
- ¼ cup (½ stick) unsalted butter, softened
- Salt and freshly ground black pepper to taste
- 1 tablespoon dried thyme

Combine the marinade ingredients in a bowl. Put the venison in a large shallow roasting pan and pour the marinade over it. Cover and refrigerate overnight, turning and basting the meat several times.

Preheat the oven to 450° F.

Remove the venison and discard the marinade; pat the venison dry. Place it on a rack in a shallow roasting pan. Rub it well with the softened butter, salt and pepper, and thyme. Roast the venison for 10 minutes; then lower the oven temperature to 350° F. and continue cooking for approximately 1 hour more, about 12 to 15 minutes per pound; a meat thermometer should register 135° F. for rare. Baste occasionally with a little more melted butter. Transfer the saddle to a warm platter, cover loosely with aluminum foil, and let rest in a warm place for 10 minutes before carving. Reserve the pan drippings to make the sauce.

Serve from a platter and pass Currant Sauce (page 176) separately.

"**F**ew of us are adventurous in the matter of food; in fact, most of us think there is something disgusting in a bill of fare to which we are unused."
WILLIAM JAMES

The new meat and potatoes:
roast young saddle of venison
with currant sauce
served with potatoes au gratin

*Brandied oranges topped with
toasted almonds and cream*

CURRANT SAUCE

MAKES 2½ CUPS

½ cup dry red wine
2 to 3 tablespoons finely
   chopped shallots
2 cups beef or veal stock,
   preferably homemade
2 tablespoons currant jelly
½ cup fresh currants
   (optional)

1 tablespoon cassis
2 tablespoons unsalted
   butter
2 teaspoons freshly squeezed
   lemon juice
Salt and freshly ground
   black pepper to taste

Pour off all the fat and deglaze the roasting pan with the red wine; then add the shallots and cook until a syrup is formed. Add the stock and reduce by two-thirds over high heat. Add the jelly, fresh currants, and cassis. Simmer gently for 5 minutes and whisk in the butter a little at a time. Correct the seasoning with the lemon juice and salt and pepper. Serve the sauce in a warm pitcher or sauce boat.

POTATOES AU GRATIN

SERVES 6

4 tablespoons unsalted butter
2 tablespoons minced shallots
2 pounds boiling potatoes,
   peeled, sliced ⅛ thick (6 to
   8 medium-size potatoes)
1 teaspoon salt, or to taste

1 cup shredded Gruyère or
   Swiss cheese
1½ cups heavy cream
3 large egg yolks
⅛ teaspoon cayenne pepper
2 to 3 tablespoons fresh
   bread crumbs

Coat a shallow 9- or 10-inch oval or square baking dish with 1 tablespoon of the butter. Preheat the oven to 350° F. or cook the dish in the same oven as the venison.

Melt 1 tablespoon of the remaining butter in a skillet and sauté the shallots until tender but not brown. Arrange layers of potatoes in the baking dish; season each layer with shallots, salt, and a sprinkling of cheese. End with a layer of cheese.

Combine the cream, egg yolks, and cayenne in a bowl. Pour over the potatoes. Sprinkle with the bread crumbs and dot with the remaining 2 tablespoons of butter. Bake for 1 to 1¼ hours or until the potatoes are tender.

"Pray for peace and grace and spiritual food, for wisdom and guidance, for all these are good, but don't forget the potatoes."

JOHN TYLER PETEE
Prayer and Potatoes

SAUTÉED WATERCRESS

SERVES 6

3 tablespoons unsalted butter
3 to 4 bunches watercress
   with tough stems removed,
   washed

1 garlic clove, smashed and
   peeled

Melt 2 tablespoons of the butter in a large skillet. Add the watercress and sauté over medium-high heat for 1 to 2 minutes or until just wilted. Then add the additional tablespoon of butter, if you wish. Place the smashed garlic clove on the prongs of a fork and whisk it through the wilted greens, just to flavor them. Discard the garlic and serve immediately.

BRANDIED ORANGES
WITH BURNT SUGAR AND ALMONDS

SERVES 6

½ cup granulated sugar
8 to 10 navel oranges
¼ cup brandy or Grand
   Marnier

½ cup slivered almonds,
   toasted
1 cup whipping cream
2 tablespoons confectioners'
   sugar

In a small heavy-bottomed saucepan, melt the sugar with 1 tablespoon of water over medium heat. Do not stir. Holding the handle of the saucepan, tilt and swirl the sugar around in the pan until it caramelizes and turns a golden brown. Pour the sugar onto a baking sheet lined with a piece of aluminum foil, shiny side up. Tilt the baking sheet to spread the melted sugar to a thickness of ¼ inch. Allow to harden at room temperature. Then break into bite-size pieces.

Peel the oranges, removing all the pith and seeds; then separate them into sections. Marinate the oranges in the brandy for at least 30 minutes, turning once.

Whip the cream with the confectioners' sugar until soft peaks form.

To assemble, divide the oranges and brandy among 6 serving dishes or tall wide-mouth wineglasses. Top the oranges with some toasted almonds and a generous dollop of cream, sprinkle with burnt sugar, and decorate with a few more almonds.

"... Some of us who, considering cooking an art, feel that a way of cooking can produce something that approaches an aesthetic emotion. What more can one say? If one had the choice of again hearing Packmann play the two Chopin sonatas or dining once more at the Café Anglais, which would one choose?"

ALICE B. TOKLAS
The Alice B. Toklas Cookbook

THE NEW MEAT AND POTATOES

A
Christmas Eve
Tradition

Most families have their own time-honored holiday feasts. When I was a child in Virginia, the meal most heavily weighted with traditional fare was reserved for Christmas Eve, and this menu, with some modifications, is what we used to have on that magical night so filled with expectancy and excitement. For me, nostalgia will always surround this dinner built around a rich and creamy oyster stew and biscuits stuffed with pungent Smithfield ham.

These classic American recipes have moved with me around the country. In Long Island, New York, I had estimable oysters from the local Atlantic waters to replace the Chesapeake Bay variety of my childhood; here in California I use Portuguese oysters raised commercially in the Pacific. And, wherever I am, I wait eagerly for a special Christmas package from my mother that always contains a country-cured Smithfield ham, a big, old moldy-looking thing that speaks a primitive language all its own. The Williamsburg cake is a traditional cake of the Colonial capital, very simple, and good at any time of the year.

Elegant in character, though far from fussy, this dinner looks best dressed up with your good china and silver. You can serve the meal by courses, or you can do as my family did and put everything out at once on a table decorated with holiday trimmings.

M·e·n·u

HOT AND SPICY ALMONDS

·

OYSTER STEW

·

SWEET POTATO BISCUITS
WITH SMITHFIELD HAM

·

WINTER SALAD
IN ROSY VINAIGRETTE

·

WILLIAMSBURG
ORANGE CAKE

·

ASSORTED CHRISTMAS COOKIES
AND CANDIES

OPPOSITE: Begin the festivities with hot and spicy almonds and a sip or two of fine sherry.

179

When first confronted with this elegant dish as a small child, I made a habit of picking out the succulent oysters and filled up instead on the creamy broth and oyster crackers. I've since grown wiser and now I savor every bite.

The delicate sweet flavor of oysters needs little embellishment. Don't forget to warm the soup bowls.

ORDER OF PREPARATION

With an hour or so of work the night before or in the morning, you can breeze through this dinner. There is really very little cooking and you can, if you like, assemble virtually everything in advance. The nuts will keep for weeks, so roast them whenever you have a few spare minutes.

The first thing to do is make the cake. If you do this in advance, keep it well wrapped in aluminum foil and wait until an hour or so before dinner to ice it. You can bake the sweet potatoes for the biscuits in the same oven as the cake. Next make the biscuits; reheat them, stuffed, before serving. Wash the greens, and mix the salad dressing. Assemble the biscuits and ham. Prepare the stew (this takes only minutes) just before you are ready to sit down—otherwise the oysters will be overcooked. Serve the cake along with any Christmas cookies and candies you have on hand.

Wine suggestions: Start the evening off with a pale dry sherry. Drink a rich, full-bodied Chardonnay Special Cuvee with the oyster stew.

HOT AND SPICY ALMONDS

MAKES 3 CUPS

1/4 cup (1/2 stick) unsalted butter	1 teaspoon garlic powder
2 tablespoons Worcestershire sauce	1/2 teaspoon cayenne pepper
1 teaspoon ground cumin	3 cups whole natural almonds
1/2 teaspoon sugar	Coarse salt to taste

Preheat the oven to 350° F.

Melt the butter in a medium-size saucepan. Add the remaining ingredients, except the almonds and coarse salt. Cook over low heat for 2 to 3 minutes. Add the nuts and stir to coat evenly with the seasonings.

Spread the nuts on an ungreased baking sheet and toast for 15 minutes, turning occasionally. Remove from the oven and toss with the coarse salt. Cool.

The nuts will keep for several weeks stored in an airtight container.

OYSTER STEW

SERVES 6

6 cups milk	Salt and freshly ground white pepper to taste
2 cups half-and-half	6 tablespoons unsalted butter
2 pints fresh oysters with their liquor	GARNISH
1 teaspoon freshly squeezed lemon juice	Chopped parsley
Tabasco sauce to taste	Oyster crackers or cold water crackers (optional)

In a medium-size saucepan, heat the milk and half-and-half to just below the boiling point, stirring to avoid scalding. Pour the oysters and their liquor, strained through a cheesecloth-lined sieve, into the milk. Heat until the edges of the oysters just begin to curl, about 2 minutes. Season with lemon juice, Tabasco sauce, and salt and pepper. Serve in hot soup bowls. Garnish each bowl with a tablespoon of butter cut into small pieces and some chopped parsley. Pass the crackers if you wish.

SWEET POTATO BISCUITS
WITH SMITHFIELD HAM

MAKES SIXTEEN 3-INCH BISCUITS

2 medium-size sweet
   potatoes, baked, peeled,
   and mashed
¼ cup packed dark brown
   sugar
3 cups all-purpose flour
1½ tablespoons baking
   powder
½ teaspoon salt
1 teaspoon ground
   cinnamon
½ teaspoon ground nutmeg
½ teaspoon ground mace
1 teaspoon grated lemon
   rind
1 cup (2 sticks) unsalted
   butter, softened
¼ cup milk
1¼ to 1½ pounds Smithfield
   ham, sliced razor thin

Preheat the oven to 450° F.

In a blender or food processor, purée the sweet potato pulp with the brown sugar until smooth.

In a bowl, sift together the flour, baking powder, salt, cinnamon, nutmeg, and mace. Mix in the lemon rind. Cut in the butter with a pastry blender until it resembles coarse meal. Add the sweet potato purée and milk and mix until just blended. Gather into a ball, turn out onto a lightly floured surface, and knead two or three times. Flatten to a thickness of ¾ inch.

Cut out the biscuits using a 3-inch-round cookie cutter lightly dipped in flour. Prick the top of the biscuits evenly in three places with a fork. Arrange ½ inch apart on an ungreased baking sheet. Bake for 12 to 15 minutes or until golden brown.

Split the biscuits and put slices of the ham inside the biscuits and serve warm. Biscuits and ham can be put together ahead of time, wrapped in aluminum foil, and reheated in a warm oven for 10 minutes.

One of the nice things about biscuits is their ease of preparation. Just remember to keep a light touch when blending the liquid and dry ingredients. The ham that you don't use for this recipe will gradually disappear in the days and weeks after the holiday.

SMITHFIELD HAM: This is the true Virginia ham named for the little town of Smithfield, Virginia, since the 1920s a packing center for country hams. The Smithfield hams come from the breed of hog called "razorbacks." These pigs are allowed to roam wild from the time they are 9 months old, feeding on local acorns and hickory nuts. They are then fattened on a diet of peanuts and corn. The hams, not pretty to look at, are aged to a dark color for no less than a year. Heavily smoked over hardwood fires stoked with apple, red oak, and hickory wood, the meat is rich, dry, pepper-coated, and salty.

Smithfield hams are available through the mail from Gwaltney Ham, P.O. Box 489, Smithfield, Virginia 23430. An average cooked ham retails for about $50.

Beware of imitations. There are country hams cured in Virginia that are nothing like the real thing. If you can't get a Smithfield, try some good prosciutto or Westphalian ham.

Oyster stew, sweet potato biscuits, and a fresh tart salad—dishes that say "home" to me

ABOVE: Sweet potato biscuits with spicy Smithfield ham complement the oyster stew perfectly.

BELOW: A Williamsburg orange cake completes this classic Southern Christmas supper.

WINTER SALAD IN ROSY VINAIGRETTE

SERVES 6

2 medium Belgian endive
1 bunch watercress
1 small head radicchio

2 large grapefruit, peeled, all
    membrane removed, and
    sectioned
1 medium avocado, peeled
    and thinly sliced

Wash and dry the greens. Arrange the salad on individual serving plates alternating the grapefruit sections and avocado slices on a bed of endive and radicchio. Garnish with sprigs of watercress. Drizzle enough dressing over the salads to coat them lightly.

ROSY VINAIGRETTE

MAKES ABOUT 1 CUP

1 garlic clove, peeled and
    minced
2 tablespoons minced fresh
    parsley
1 teaspoon honey
⅔ cup olive oil

2 tablespoons raspberry
    vinegar
2 tablespoons freshly
    squeezed orange juice
Salt and freshly ground
    black pepper to taste

Whisk together the garlic, parsley, honey, and olive oil. Add the vinegar and orange juice, whisking constantly until the dressing is blended. Adjust the seasoning with salt and pepper.

The rosy-orange vinaigrette looks pretty on the pale grapefruit and avocado slices and its slightly sweet taste complements the acidity of the fruit.

WILLIAMSBURG ORANGE CAKE

SERVES 6 TO 8

1 medium-size orange,
    washed
¾ cup sugar
½ cup (1 stick) unsalted
    butter, softened
2 large eggs, beaten
1 teaspoon sherry
1 cup buttermilk

2 cups all-purpose flour
1 teaspoon baking soda
½ teaspoon salt
1 cup currants
½ cup coarsely chopped
    pecans

*Williamsburg Icing with
Sherry (recipe follows)*

Preheat the oven to 350° F. Generously butter a 9 × 9 × 2-inch pan. Line the bottom of the pan with wax paper; then butter the wax paper. Set aside.

With a sharp knife remove the peel from the orange. Be sure to discard all the bitter white pith. Reserve a 2 × 2-inch piece of the orange peel for the icing.

In a blender or a food processor fitted with the metal blade, finely mince the remaining orange peel with half of the sugar. Transfer to a mixing bowl.

A classic American cake from Colonial Williamsburg.

Cream the butter with the remaining sugar until light and fluffy. Add the eggs, one at a time, beating well after each addition. Add the sherry and buttermilk and continue beating until well mixed.

To the minced orange rind and sugar add the flour, baking soda, salt, and currants. Toss to coat the currants with the flour.

Gradually beat the liquid ingredients into the dry ingredients. Mix until smooth. Add the pecans and mix until they are evenly distributed in the batter.

Pour into the prepared pan and bake for 30 to 35 minutes or until a cake tester inserted near the center comes out clean. Cool the cake in the pan for 10 minutes; then turn out onto a wire rack, remove the paper, and cool completely before spreading the icing over the top and sides of the cake.

WILLIAMSBURG ICING WITH SHERRY

*1 2 × 2-inch piece orange
peel (reserved from the cake
recipe)*
2 cups confectioners' sugar

*5 tablespoons unsalted butter,
softened*
1 large egg white
1 to 2 tablespoons dry sherry

In a food processor fitted with a metal blade or in a blender, mince the reserved piece of orange peel with 1 cup of the confectioners' sugar. Transfer to a mixing bowl. Add the remaining cup of confectioners' sugar and gradually beat in the softened butter. Add the egg white and continue beating until thick but smooth. Add enough sherry, starting with 1 tablespoon, to make the frosting of spreading consistency.

"It's always
the same: a morning arrives in November,
and my friend, as though officially
inaugurating the Christmas time of year that
exhilarates her imagination and fuels the
blaze of her heart, announces: 'It's fruitcake
weather! Fetch our buggy. Help me
find my hat.' "
TRUMAN CAPOTE
A Christmas Memory

A CHRISTMAS EVE TRADITION

*Endive with crème fraîche and golden
caviar—a terrific Hail and Farewell*

New Year's Eve

*T*ime passes, we all know it, but one
of the few times we actually take account of it is on New Year's Eve, and
even then, we do not like to stare the melancholy fact dead in the eye.
Instead, we are inclined to note the passing of the old year and herald
the arrival of the new with a lot of noise, alcohol, and other people. But
let it be said: There is another way. If you have announced too many
times, "I hate going out to a big, noisy party on New Year's Eve," you
can avoid the situation and turn things to your advantage by having
some like-minded friends over for a festive but civilized late dinner. Just
keep a few funny hats and noisemakers on hand should the almost
inevitable wave of sentiment carry you in its wake at the approach of the
midnight hour.

This is a celebration dinner—with a strong Italian accent. If your
guests arrive wearing tuxedos or a jewel or two, they will not be over-
dressed for this menu. Lasagne, a plain dish and one of the first the
nervous cook learns to make to please a crowd, scales lofty new heights
in this elegant version with wild mushrooms. It is not easy to make a
good lasagne. Its many steps take some trouble (the flavors must be put
together so that they blend and harmonize), but it does have the great
advantage of allowing early-in-the-day assembly; just pop it in the oven
when the festivities get under way. This is dinner for six, but the lasagne
can readily be expanded to feed a larger crowd.

A mouthwatering serving of wild mushroom lasagne— a surprisingly elegant main dish

Do you remember those inconsequential tortonis in demure paper cups you ordered long ago to round out your first Italian restaurant experiences? Well, the lustrous tortoni bombe presented here—turned out of an Italianate dome-shaped mold—is a far cry from its ancestral namesake. It is sensuous, sophisticated, enormously rich and, yes, fattening. Enjoy—and Happy New Year!

ORDER OF PREPARATION

*T*here's quite a lot of work here but much can be done well in advance and this *is* a week when one often has a little extra time off. One special word of caution: Be sure your freezer will freeze ice cream *hard*—or the bombe will be a bomb. Make the bombe at least 24 hours in advance.

Make the Florentines and assemble the lasagne the day ahead or in the morning and chill. Or do both the afternoon of the dinner. The lasagne takes about an hour to assemble and 25 minutes to cook.

With these out of the way, you are finished with preparation until an hour or so before your guests arrive. If you have made the lasagne ahead, remove it from the refrigerator and bring it to room temperature before baking. Assemble the caviar and endive no more than 30 minutes before the first arrivals and keep refrigerated. They are so simple to do, you can make them up at the last moment. The broccoli rabe takes about 15 minutes; do just before you are ready to eat. Unmold the bombe just before serving. Pour the espresso and pass the cookies.

Wine suggestions: Toast the new year with a fine Champagne. And with dinner, serve one of California's best Cabernet Sauvignons.

*E*ndive and caviar are both expensive, but, in this hors d'oeuvre for six, a little goes a long way.

ENDIVE WITH CRÈME FRAÎCHE AND GOLDEN CAVIAR

SERVES 6

2 short fat heads Belgian
  endive
½ cup crème fraîche or
  sour cream

1½ ounces golden caviar
GARNISH
  Several dill sprigs

Trim the bottoms of the endive so that the leaves are about the same length. Beat the crème fraîche until smooth. Neatly arrange the endive leaves on a platter. Put about ½ teaspoon of crème fraîche on the bottom of each leaf and top with a few grains of caviar. Garnish with the dill sprigs if desired. Keep refrigerated until ready to serve.

WILD MUSHROOM LASAGNE

SERVES 6

1 ounce dried porcini
  mushrooms
2 pounds fresh mushrooms,
  well cleaned
¼ cup olive oil
¼ cup (½ stick) unsalted
  butter
1 medium-size onion, finely
  chopped
1 14½-ounce can Italian
  plum tomatoes, drained
  and coarsely chopped
¼ cup chopped fresh Italian
  parsley
  Salt and freshly ground
  black pepper to taste

1 1-pound box lasagne
  noodles
BÉCHAMEL SAUCE
½ cup (1 stick) unsalted
  butter
⅓ cup all-purpose flour
4 cups milk
1 teaspoon ground nutmeg
½ teaspoon salt

6 ounces prosciutto, thinly
  sliced
¼ pound Parmesan cheese,
  freshly grated
2 tablespoons unsalted
  butter

Bring 4 quarts of water to a rapid boil with 1 tablespoon of salt.

Soak the dried mushrooms for at least 30 minutes in 2 cups of warm water. Coarsely chop the fresh mushrooms by hand (the food processor will extract too much liquid).

In a large skillet, heat the oil and butter; then add the fresh mushrooms and cook over medium-high heat until all the liquid has been released and has evaporated. With a slotted spoon, carefully remove the reconstituted porcini mushrooms from the water. Reserve the water. Rinse the mushrooms thoroughly and chop them coarsely. Add the porcini, onion, tomatoes, and parsley to the skillet. Pour the mushroom-soaking liquid through a small sieve lined with paper towels into the skillet. Partially cover the pan and cook until the liquid has evaporated. Season with salt and pepper.

Preheat the oven to 425° F.

When the 4 quarts of water begin to boil, add the pasta strips one at a time, until all are in the pot. Bring to a boil again and cook for 5 to 7 minutes. Drain and immediately rinse each pasta strip under cold running water to prevent sticking. Lay them out on paper towels to drain.

Melt the butter for the sauce in a small saucepan. Add the flour gradually and stir for 3 to 5 minutes over low heat. Slowly stir in the milk. Cook and stir over medium heat until thickened and smooth, about 8 to 10 minutes. Season with nutmeg and salt.

Liberally butter an 8½ × 10½-inch lasagne pan. Line the bottom of the pan with a slightly overlapping layer of pasta strips. Spread a third of the mushroom mixture over the pasta, top with one quarter of the béchamel sauce and a sprinkling of the Parmesan cheese. Cover with slices of the proscuitto and repeat the sequence two more times. Cover with one last layer of pasta, top with the remaining béchamel sauce and Parmesan, and dot with the 2 tablespoons of butter, cut into small pieces.

Bake for 20 to 25 minutes or until the cheese is melted and golden brown on top. Allow to stand for 10 minutes before serving.

"**E**gg
of an hour, bread of a day, wine of a year,
a friend of thirty years."
ITALIAN PROVERB

"**D**um
vivimus vivamus.—Let us live while
we live."
UNATTRIBUTED

Broccoli rabe (also called rapini or raab) has both a bitter and spicy quality, perfect after the rich lasagne. A variety of broccoli, it has long, thick leaves topped with miniature pale green broccoli buds. If not available substitute one of the salads from this book.

BROCCOLI RABE
WITH GARLIC, LEMON, AND OIL

SERVES 6

1 tablespoon salt
3 pounds broccoli rabe, trimmed
1/4 cup extra virgin olive oil
1 tablespoon minced garlic
Juice of 1 lemon

Salt and freshly ground black pepper to taste
GARNISH
1 small head radicchio
Lemon wedges

Bring 3 to 4 quarts water to a boil and add the salt. Blanch the broccoli for 3 to 5 minutes, depending on thickness and tenderness. Drain and immediately plunge into ice water to stop the cooking. Drain and pat dry. Heat the oil in a medium-size saucepan and sauté the garlic until lightly colored.

Arrange the greens on a warm platter and coat evenly with the oil and garlic. Sprinkle with the lemon juice and season with salt and freshly ground pepper.

Garnish the platter with a few radicchio leaves and lemon wedges. Serve warm or at room temperature.

TORTONI BOMBE

SERVES 6

1 cup finely chopped candied orange peel
1/4 cup dark rum
1/2 cup unblanched almonds
3 pints vanilla ice cream or gelato, softened to a stiff spreading consistency

1/4 cup whipping cream
3/4 cup toasted unsweetened coconut
1/4 cup grated semi-sweet chocolate

Turn your freezer up to high. Put a 6-cup ice-cream mold in the freezer. Soak the candied fruit in the rum for 30 minutes. Toast the almonds in a 350° F. oven for 10 minutes or until golden; coarsely chop. Drain the candied fruit.

Combine the softened ice cream and the candied fruit and spread evenly over the inside of the mold. Refreeze immediately. When frozen solid remove from the freezer and scoop out 1 cup of ice cream from the center of the mold, leaving a wide, thick edge all around. Reserve the cup of ice cream and return both to the freezer. Whip the cream until stiff. Fold in half the coconut, half the almonds, and the chocolate. Fill the scooped-out center with this mixture. Use the reserved ice cream to cover the filling and to make a thick bottom layer. Refreeze until very firm.

To serve, fill a large bowl with tepid water. Dip the frozen mold into the water for 8 to 10 seconds and invert onto a serving platter. Decorate with the remaining coconut and almonds. Serve immediately.

"**H**ere's
to the present—and to hell with the past!
A health to the future and joy to the last."
UNATTRIBUTED

FLORENTINES

MAKES 2½ DOZEN COOKIES

3 ounces candied orange
  peel, finely chopped
6 ounces blanched almonds,
  finely chopped
⅓ cup all-purpose flour
3 tablespoons unsalted
  butter

¾ cup heavy cream
½ cup sugar
2 tablespoons light corn
  syrup
½ teaspoon vanilla extract

Tortoni bombe and florentines are a spectacular finish to a fine supper—and a spectacular start to a New Year.

Preheat the oven to 350° F. Line a baking sheet with parchment paper.

Combine the candied orange peel, almonds, and flour in a mixing bowl and toss.

In a medium-size saucepan, bring to a boil the butter, cream, sugar, and corn syrup, stirring constantly until it reaches 240° F. on a candy thermometer. Remove from the heat and stir in the vanilla and dry ingredients. The batter will be slightly runny. Drop by heaping tablespoons onto the prepared baking sheet 1 inch apart. Smooth the tops with the back of the spoon. Bake for 10 to 12 minutes or until golden. Cool completely before removing from the baking sheet.

Store the Florentines between layers of wax paper in an airtight container.

NEW YEAR'S EVE

Pulling in the Purse Strings

My theme here is a simple one: economy. This is a very inexpensive meal, tailored to those lean weeks that sadly but inevitably follow the massive expenditures of the holiday season. Standard fare in almost all classic peasant cuisines, oxtails are inexpensive, readily available, and delicious. Derived from beef cattle, not oxen, they have the hearty flavor of meat that lies close to the bones and joints, and the high glutinous content of the tailbone yields, after long simmering, a supremely rich and nourishing broth perfect on cold winter evenings. The other components of the dinner—pasta, leeks, carrots, and oranges—won't set you back either.

Cooking *en daube* is a method of braising meat in red wine and herbs. A *daubiere* is a type of closed casserole used to make this stew. Since the daube of oxtails is a close cousin of the Italian ossobuco, I have borrowed the classic garnish for that dish, gremolada, for an accent.

ORDER OF PREPARATION

Like the veal ragout (on page 200), the daube takes time to make. In fact, it benefits from being made a day ahead; the flavor intensifies and you can lessen the calorie count by removing any fat that, with refrigeration, congeals on the top.

Put the oranges in the freezer the night or the morning before the dinner. If you are baking the cookies yourself, make them while the daube is cooking. With the daube and dessert out of the way, you don't have to think about dinner until an hour before your guests arrive.

Bring the daube to room temperature. Wash the leeks, braise them, and get them ready for the broiler. Make the gremolada. Grate the carrots and start a pot of water to boil for the egg noodles. Place the daube in a low oven to warm for 45 minutes to 1 hour. Remove the oranges from the freezer. Broil the leeks just as people come to the table. Remove the first course and finish the noodles and carrots. Serve the daube on a big platter surrounded by the noodles. Pass the carrots separately.

Wine suggestion: A rich, complex Merlot would complement the subtle harmony of the oxtail daube.

BRAISED LEEKS

SERVES 6

3½ pounds leeks
  (approximately 6 to 8
  medium-size leeks)
  Freshly squeezed lemon
  juice
¼ cup unseasoned bread
  crumbs, toasted

3 tablespoons freshly grated
  Parmesan cheese
2 tablespoons unsalted
  butter, cut into small
  pieces
  Freshly ground white
  pepper

Trim the leeks about 6 inches long. Make a slit lengthwise, halfway through each leek, to clean the center. Hold under cold running water, rinsing out all the dirt. Arrange the leeks in a single layer in a large saucepan and add enough water to cover. Cover, bring to a boil, and simmer for 8 to 10 minutes or until just tender. Drain and pat dry. Transfer the leeks to a buttered baking dish. Squeeze a little lemon juice over the top and sprinkle with the Parmesan cheese and bread crumbs. Dot with the butter. Broil for 2 to 3 minutes or until the cheese melts. Serve with freshly ground white pepper.

OXTAIL DAUBE WITH GREMOLADA

SERVES 6

5½ to 6 pounds oxtails,
  trimmed of all excess fat
  (see Note)
  Salt and freshly ground
  black pepper to taste
½ cup lard or vegetable oil
2 garlic cloves, peeled and
  minced
4 medium-size onions,
  coarsely chopped
1 carrot, peeled and
  coarsely chopped

1½ cups coarsely chopped
  celery
1 bottle dry red wine
1 cup water or beef stock
  Bouquet garni of several
  parsley sprigs, 1 thyme
  sprig, and 1 bay leaf tied
  in a square of cheesecloth

Gremolada (page 195)

"**F**rom behind my oven I feel the ugly edifice of routine crumbling beneath my hands."
CARÊME

*T*reated to a long simmer in a closed pot, the oxtails become very tender. Do not let them boil. Gremolada is the traditional Italian garnish for ossobuco. It is quite pungent in taste, so you might want to experiment with the quantity before adding the full amount.

Oxtail daube with gremolada, parsley egg noodles, and sizzling carrots—all economical, yet all very delicious

Preheat the oven to 325° F.

Sprinkle the oxtails with salt and pepper. In a large heavy skillet, heat the fat and brown the oxtails on all sides in batches over medium-high heat. As they brown, transfer them to a large flameproof casserole.

Pour off all but 2 tablespoons of fat from the skillet, and, over medium heat, sauté the garlic, onion, carrot, and celery, stirring occasionally, until they are lightly colored. Transfer the vegetables to the casserole, draining off as much fat as possible by pressing them against the side of the skillet before removing.

Deglaze the skillet with 1 cup of the red wine and reduce to a glaze. Add the remaining wine and 1 cup of water or beef stock. Bring to a boil and pour over the oxtails and vegetables. Add the bouquet garni, cover the casserole, and place in the middle of the oven. Bake for 2½ to 3 hours without stirring. The meat should be very tender and come easily off the bone.

Carefully remove the oxtails to a platter, cover, and keep warm. Discard the cooked vegetables, strain the liquid into a degreasing cup, and pour off all the fat. You may need to do this in several batches. Pour the degreased liquid into a saucepan and bring to a boil; reduce by one-third.

Wipe out the casserole and add the oxtails and the liquid. The daube may be covered and refrigerated at this point. If you refrigerate the dish overnight the daube will benefit from a second degreasing. Remove any congealed fat from the top of the sauce and let it stand at room temperature for 30 minutes before proceeding.

Preheat the oven to 325° F. and heat the daube for 45 minutes to 1 hour or until the meat is heated throughout. Do not boil.

Add half the gremolada 15 minutes before serving. To serve, place one or two oxtails, depending on size, and some sauce on each plate. Garnish with additional gremolada.

NOTE: When buying oxtails, look for 2- to 3-inch-wide joints, with as little fat as possible. The smaller, fatty joints can be tough and without flavor.

Frozen oranges and gingersnap stars, one of my all-time favorite cookies

GREMOLADA

1 tablespoon grated lemon rind
3 tablespoons chopped fresh parsley

3 garlic cloves, peeled and
    finely minced

Combine all the ingredients in a small bowl.

PARSLEY EGG NOODLES

SERVES 6

1½ pounds fresh or dried
    wide egg noodles
4 tablespoons unsalted
    butter

3 to 4 tablespoons finely
    chopped fresh parsley
Salt and freshly ground
    black pepper to taste

*H*omemade fresh noodles are easy to make, taking about an hour. But now there are so many pasta shops and gourmet stores selling their own fresh pasta that it is simpler to take this route. Buy plenty. Tightly wrapped in rigid plastic containers, they will keep forever in the freezer.

Cook the noodles in a large pot of salted boiling water until al dente. Drain well.

Melt the butter in the same pot, add the noodles and toss well, coating completely. Add some parsley, season well with salt and pepper, and stir constantly until very hot. Serve garnished with the remaining parsley.

This recipe is the invention of Devon Fredericks, my good friend and a great cook.

SIZZLING CARROTS

SERVES 6

3 tablespoons unsalted butter
6 cups grated carrots (about
6 to 8 large carrots)
Pinch of sugar

Salt and freshly ground
black pepper to taste
1 tablespoon finely chopped
fresh parsley

In a large skillet, melt the butter over medium heat. Add the carrots and sugar and sauté for 8 to 10 minutes or until soft and slightly golden. Season with salt and pepper and garnish with the chopped parsley.

FINE STORE-BOUGHT SNAPS: I am a big cookie lover (they were the first thing I learned to make) and I've included quite a few recipes for them in this book. If you don't share my enthusiasm for baking them, buy Fox's Gingersnap Biscuits for this dinner. They are very thin, crisp ginger cookies that come in a short red carton from England. They are available in gourmet stores.

GINGERSNAP STARS

MAKES 3 DOZEN COOKIES

1/3 cup molasses
6 tablespoons unsalted
butter
1/3 cup packed dark brown
sugar
1 1/4 cups sifted all-purpose
flour

1/4 teaspoon salt
1 teaspoon baking soda
1 tablespoon ground
ginger
1/2 teaspoon ground
cinnamon
1/2 teaspoon ground cloves

Melt the molasses with the butter and sugar in a saucepan over medium heat. Cool. Combine the flour, salt, baking soda, and spices in a mixing bowl. Gradually stir in the molasses mixture until well blended. The dough will be slightly soft. Divide it into two parts and refrigerate until well chilled and firm, at least 30 minutes.

Preheat the oven to 350° F.

Cover baking sheets with aluminum foil, shiny side up. Remove one batch of dough from the refrigerator and roll it out on a lightly floured board as thin as possible, cut with a floured star-shaped cutter or stencil and place 1 inch apart on the prepared baking sheet. Bake for 12 to 15 minutes; remove to a wire rack to cool. Repeat with the remaining dough, gathering scraps and chilling before rolling again.

Icy cold and very refreshing. I found these first in the freezer of my friend Emile di Antonio, the film director.

FROZEN ORANGES

SERVES 6

6 medium-size navel oranges or tangelos
(Try to buy seedless ones if possible.)

Wash the oranges and pat them dry. Place them in the freezer for several hours or overnight. Remove the fruit approximately 30 minutes before serving. (They should be served partially thawed.) Slice off the tops with a sharp knife and eat the inside with a spoon or peel and cut into slices.

TV
Dinner

When winter weather is at its dreariest and most persistent, gather your friends together before the TV on a weekend night and dispel the general gloom with this comforting dinner as you take in some worthy or unworthy media event. The VCR comes into its own on these baleful evenings, as does a sound one-pot dinner. Though casual in spirit, a true "TV dinner" this is not. You will have puttered in and out of the kitchen during the day to prepare it and the result, prettily displayed around the coffee table or on individual flat baskets, owes more to the cuisine of provincial France than it does to the heartless purveyors of those sectioned aluminum platters from the frozen food aisle of the supermarket.

A well-crafted stew is nothing like the improvised throw-everything-in-the-pot solution to the leftover problem, and it should not be undertaken in too light a humor. Its several steps require attention and care. Two secrets: Brown the meat properly and do not crowd the pieces in the pan; strain out and discard the sauce vegetables from the stock (the vegetables for the ragout are cooked separately and then reheated in the sauce). Prepared this way the ragout has such a fine rich flavor that it satisfies with nothing more than a salad and some crusty bread to soak up the sauce. Make a lot if you want to have extra for a dinner later on in a hurried week.

M·e·n·u

SALAD OF CELERIAC, CELERY,
AND GRUYÈRE
IN COARSE MUSTARD SAUCE

·

RAGOUT OF VEAL
WITH WINTER ROOT
VEGETABLES

·

ROASTED GARLIC
ON TOASTED FRENCH BREAD

·

PEAR PASTIS

ORDER OF PREPARATION

*T*he ragout can be made in advance, up to the point of adding the vegetables, and finished off at the last minute.

While the veal is cooking, make the pastis. It takes about 30 minutes to assemble and another 30 minutes to bake. During the ragout's final hour of cooking time, cook the vegetables you will add to it later, roast the garlic in the same oven, and toast some slices of French bread. Prepare the salad and refrigerate it. When you serve the ragout, put the pastis in the oven to warm slightly. Dust with confectioners' sugar just before serving.

Go to the trouble of making up individual trays or large flat baskets for each guest. Not everything has to match. A large cloth napkin for the lap is essential, and it's nice for everyone to have his or her own individual salt and pepper. Have a fire blazing if you have a fireplace. Flowers on the coffee table or a side table will put winter even further at bay.

Wine suggestion: Serve a refreshing Chardonnay.

SALAD OF CELERIAC, CELERY, AND GRUYÈRE IN COARSE MUSTARD SAUCE

SERVES 6

1 large celeriac (celery root), peeled and cut into julienne strips
6 large tender stalks celery, cut into julienne strips
¼ pound Gruyère cheese, cut into julienne strips
1 cup mayonnaise

1 tablespoon coarse Dijon mustard
Juice of 1 lemon
Salt and freshly ground black pepper to taste
½ cup finely minced mixed herbs, such as parsley, dill, tarragon, or chives
6 large Bibb lettuce leaves

Bring 6 cups of salted water to a boil; blanch the celeriac for 10 seconds, no more —it should still be slightly crunchy. Refresh under cold running water; then pat dry.

Toss the celeriac, celery, and Gruyère strips together in a bowl. In another bowl, combine the mayonnaise, mustard, lemon juice, and salt and pepper. Add the dressing to the vegetable mixture and mix well. Stir in the herbs, cover, and refrigerate until ready to serve. Serve on individual plates on a bed of Bibb lettuce.

A rich, delectable, and tangy salad

ABOVE: Ragout of veal with roasted garlic and bread—a perfect cozy winter meal

BELOW: The pear pastis: a subtle, warming—and sophisticated—dessert

RAGOUT OF VEAL
WITH WINTER ROOT VEGETABLES

SERVES 6

3 pounds lean, boneless
 stewing veal, cut into
 1½-inch cubes
½ cup all-purpose flour
 Salt and freshly ground
 black pepper
4 tablespoons unsalted
 butter
2 tablespoons olive oil
½ cup brandy
3 to 4 leeks, white parts
 only, split and
 thoroughly cleaned
2 carrots, peeled and cut
 into 1-inch cubes
½ tablespoon dried thyme
1 cup dry white wine

3 cups chicken or veal
 stock, preferably
 homemade
12 small white onions,
 peeled
3 turnips, peeled
4 carrots, peeled and cut
 into 1-inch pieces
3 tablespoons unsalted
 butter
1 pound mushrooms,
 cleaned and stemmed
1 cup heavy cream
1½ tablespoons Dijon
 mustard

GARNISH
 Chopped parsley

Preheat the oven to 350° F.

Pat the veal dry and roll in a combination of the flour and salt and pepper. Shake off any excess flour. Heat 2 tablespoons of the butter and the oil over medium-high heat in a large ovenproof casserole. When the fat is hot but not smoking, brown the cubes of veal on all sides, about 5 minutes. Do this in several batches so you don't crowd the veal. Discard the oil and deglaze the pan with the brandy.

Melt the remaining 2 tablespoons of butter in the brandy and add the leeks, carrots, and thyme. Stir, cover, and cook over low heat for 10 minutes or until the vegetables are just soft. Add the white wine, stock, and veal. Bring to a simmer on top of the stove, skim off any scum that forms, cover, and bake for 1 hour to 1 hour and 15 minutes or until the veal is tender.

Remove from the oven and pour the contents of the casserole through a strainer set over a bowl to catch the stock. Save all the pieces of veal but discard the vegetables. Wipe the casserole clean and return the stock and the veal to the casserole. The ragout may be prepared to this point a day ahead and refrigerated.

Blanch the onions in salted boiling water for 3 to 4 minutes. Drain. Put the turnips, carrots, and onions in a small saucepan with 2 tablespoons of the butter, cover, and cook over medium heat for 15 to 20 minutes or until just tender.

Leave small mushrooms whole and half or quarter any larger ones.

Heat the remaining tablespoon of butter in a skillet and sauté the mushrooms for 3 to 4 minutes or just until they start to brown. Set them aside.

Remove any fat from the surface of the ragout, and scoop out the veal pieces. Set them aside. Add the heavy cream to the casserole, bring to a boil, and reduce the sauce by one third. Stir in the mustard. Return the veal to the casserole, add the vegetables, and simmer for 4 to 5 minutes or until heated through. Garnish each serving with a little chopped parsley.

ROASTED GARLIC
ON TOASTED FRENCH BREAD

SERVES 6

6 *whole garlic heads*
  Rosemary sprigs (optional)
1 *cup olive oil*

French bread, sliced and
lightly toasted

Preheat the oven to 350° F.

With a sharp knife cut about ¼ inch from the top of each garlic head. Lay a rosemary sprig over each "head." Place in a baking dish and dribble the oil evenly over all. Bake for 1 hour, basting frequently.

Serve each guest 1 garlic head accompanied by slices of lightly toasted French bread. Each guest should have a knife or small cocktail fork to remove the softened cloves of garlic to smear on the bread.

*G*arlic has been called the "truffle of Provence." Here it is roasted and smeared on French bread for an appetizer. It loses its sharp taste when roasted and becomes sweet and almost nutty. The addition of the oil makes it very spreadable.

PEAR PASTIS

SERVES 6

FILLING
2 *tablespoons unsalted butter*
6 *to 8 ripe but firm pears,*
  peeled, cored, and sliced
1 *tablespoon freshly squeezed*
  lemon juice
2 *tablespoons light brown*
  sugar
1 *tablespoon poire liqueur*
  (optional)

DOUGH
1 *1-pound box filo dough,*
  thawed according to the
  directions on the box
1 *cup (2 sticks) unsalted*
  butter, melted
½ *cup sugar*
3 *tablespoons freshly made*
  unseasoned bread crumbs
  Confectioners' sugar for
  dusting (optional)

To make the filling, melt the butter in a large skillet. Add the pear slices and lemon juice and cook for 4 to 5 minutes, stirring gently. Drain well. Toss with the sugar and liqueur. Cool.

Preheat the oven to 350° F.

Remove the filo from the package and place on a flat surface covered with wax paper. Cover the filo with a damp tea towel to prevent the sheets from drying out. Butter a 9-inch pie plate. Lay 1 sheet of filo dough on a clean work surface. Brush with melted butter and sprinkle lightly with sugar. Line the pie plate with the dough. Repeat this process with 8 more layers, placing each new sheet of filo at a slight angle to the one beneath so that the edges are irregular. Sprinkle the last sheet with the bread crumbs. Add the pear filling and cover with 9 additional sheets of filo, buttering and dusting with sugar each time. Fold in the edges to make a neat roll and brush with butter to hold in place. Butter and sugar 3 to 4 more sheets of filo and loosely crumple them on top so that they remain "puffed-up." Sprinkle with a little more sugar and bake for 25 to 30 minutes or until golden brown.

Dust with confectioners' sugar just before serving.

*T*his airy fruit pie has nothing to do with the licorice-flavored apéritif of the same name. The dessert comes from Gascony in southwest France and is itself a variation on the pastilla, a layered meat pie of Moroccan origin. Traditionally made from a paper-thin, hand-stretched dough, a pastis suffers not at all when ready-made filo dough is used instead. Resist any impulse to add more spice to the pear filling—the delicate fruit flavor is easily overpowered.

M·e·n·u

NORWEGIAN SALMON
WITH PUMPERNICKEL HEARTS

·

LOIN LAMB CHOPS
ON A BED OF RED PEPPERS
AND MINT

·

ROSE-SABLE POTATOES

·

SALAD OF BEETS, ARUGULA,
AND MONTRACHET

·

CHOCOLATE-CRANBERRY
TORTE

*ABOVE: For a romantic touch, freeze violets
in ice cubes to use in the water glasses.*

*T*his is not a feast for young lovers. Flagrant, early love rarely tastes the food it eats, if it chooses to eat at all. Pass by the head-over-heels (they can take care of themselves on this day) and, instead, invite to dinner some well-seasoned couples who love each other a lot. That's as foolproof a recipe for good company as I can think of, and these lovers are sure to savor this combination of old-fashioned and contemporary romantic dishes. Some of these foods are in fact considered aphrodisiacs (fish, arugula, chocolate), so set the stage and hope their wanton chemistry prevails.

Not a great deal of work is involved in this menu so take some time to set a pretty table. Hearts and flowers are fine, lace doilies or napkins add something special, candlesticks are a must. If you don't have a chest full of family silver, rent or borrow a few showy pieces. All the lovely things in our photograph were ready at hand in the Napa Valley home of Thomas Bartlett, where we took the pictures. Tom is a wonderful entertainer and, yes, a real sweetheart.

ORDER OF PREPARATION

*Y*ou will want to feel pampered and in a romantic mood yourself for this evening. With this in mind, I have created a menu of enticing food that can be made in very little time. You will not have to spend long hours in the kitchen before your

guests arrive. Make the cake in advance and freeze it. The buttercream will keep for several days so make it ahead and keep it refrigerated. Assemble the cake the morning of the dinner and refrigerate it.

Some other do-ahead tasks: The potato roses require some manual dexterity. Practice with a few and don't be discouraged; toothpicks or bamboo skewers can be used to hold the ribbons in place. Once they are removed, no one will be able to tell the difference. Keep the potato ribbons in ice water until you are ready to bake them. Wash the salad greens and refrigerate them; make the dressing. Toast the pine nuts and clarify the butter. Set the table.

Prepare the first course just before the guests arrive; then refrigerate it. The rest of the dinner takes about 20 minutes. Bring the salad to room temperature. Sauté the peppers and set them aside. As you serve the first course, start roasting the potatoes. Get up once to baste them. Clear the table and give your guests a glass of wine while you check the potatoes, reheat the peppers, and broil the chops. Garnish the potato roses with sprigs of watercress and each chop with mint butter. Serve immediately. Now assemble and serve the salad. Before sitting down, take the cake from the refrigerator. Serve the cake with valentines for everyone.

Wine suggestions: Toast to love with a crisp Champagne. A rich Merlot will do the lamb justice.

"**L**ove, with very young people, is heartless business. We drink at that age from thirst, or to get drunk; it is only later in life that we occupy ourselves with the individuality of our wine."
ISAK DINESEN

NORWEGIAN SALMON WITH PUMPERNICKEL HEARTS

SERVES 6

6 ounces Norwegian
  salmon, sliced very thin
3 limes
2 tablespoons freshly cracked
  coriander seeds
2 tablespoons coarsely
  chopped fresh coriander
  leaves (leave small leaves
  whole)

12 very thin slices
  pumpernickel bread (see
  Note)
2 to 3 tablespoons unsalted
  butter, softened
¼ cup finely minced fresh
  parsley

Arrange 2 to 3 slices of salmon on each individual plate. Cut 2 of the limes in half and squeeze a little juice over the salmon. Garnish the salmon with the cracked coriander seeds and chopped coriander leaves. Cut the remaining lime into paper-thin rounds and use these as another garnish.

Use a heart-shaped cookie cutter or stencil to cut 1 heart from the center of each slice of pumpernickel bread. Carefully spread the edges with a little softened butter. Dip the edges in the minced parsley to coat. Place alongside the salmon.

NOTE: The best type is the European-style black bread by Oroweat.

LOIN LAMB CHOPS ON A BED OF RED PEPPERS AND MINT

SERVES 6

2 tablespoons unsalted butter
2 tablespoons minced garlic
4 to 6 sweet red peppers,
  seeded and sliced into thin
  strips
3 tablespoons chopped fresh
  mint (see Note)

6 to 12 loin lamb chops, cut
  1 to 1¼ inches thick
  Salt and freshly ground
  black pepper
2 tablespoons unsalted butter,
  softened
GARNISH
  Whole mint leaves

In a large skillet, melt the butter and add 1 tablespoon of the garlic; cook for 1 minute, but do not let the garlic brown. Add the peppers and 2 tablespoons of mint and cook for 3 to 4 minutes longer, stirring frequently. Season with salt and freshly ground pepper to taste. Keep warm over low heat or set aside and reheat slowly.

Season the lamb chops with salt and pepper and grill or broil for 3 to 4 minutes on each side for medium-rare.

Combine the softened butter and remaining mint and garlic into a smooth paste.

Set 1 or 2 lamb chops on each plate and surround with the peppers. Garnish each chop with a teaspoon of the mint butter and additional fresh mint leaves.

NOTE: If you can't find fresh mint, fresh basil is also good.

"**W**ithout bread, without wine, love is nothing."
FRENCH PROVERB

ROSE-SABLE POTATOES

SERVES 6

6 medium-size potatoes,
   peeled and washed

1 cup (2 sticks) unsalted
   butter
Salt

Cut each potato into two 2 × 1-inch cylinders. Soak them in cold water for 30 minutes.

Preheat the oven to 425° F.

Clarify the butter over low heat. When the butter has melted, discard the foam and carefully pour the clear liquid butter into a bowl, making sure the creamy residue remains behind.

Using a very sharp paring knife, peel the potatoes in one continuous ribbon, as if you were peeling a lemon. Do not worry if the strip should break, the desired shape can still be achieved. Dip the potato ribbons in the clarified butter and roll them up to look like roses. If the strips are broken, use toothpicks or bamboo skewers to hold the shape together. Place them on a baking sheet, sprinkle lightly with salt, and bake for 15 to 20 minutes or until golden brown. Keep warm until ready to serve.

This dish is similar to one that the charming and romantic French chef, Pierre Troisgros, uses as a garnish for many of his famous entrées. The roasted potatoes emerge light chestnut brown from the oven—the color of sable.

SALAD OF BEETS, ARUGULA, AND MONTRACHET

SERVES 6

1½ to 2 pounds beets, tops
   removed
4 tablespoons walnut or
   hazelnut oil
2 tablespoons olive oil
2 tablespoons white wine
   vinegar
1 tablespoon minced
   shallots

Salt and freshly ground
   black pepper to taste
1 head arugula, torn into
   bite-size pieces
¼ pound Montrachet goat
   cheese
¼ cup toasted and coarsely
   chopped pine nuts

Preheat the oven to 400° F.

Bake the beets in a shallow baking dish for 1 hour or until tender. Let cool. Peel and cut into matchsticks.

Combine the oils, vinegar, shallots, and salt and pepper in a bowl and blend well.

Arrange the arugula on salad plates and spoon the beets in the center of each plate. Divide the dressing evenly over the salads. Crumble a little goat cheese over each serving and sprinkle with a few pine nuts.

People who know their classical literature might remember that the salad green arugula (also known as rocket) has a racy reputation. The poet Ovid warned that "chaste men should refrain from its use." The spicy green is hard to find at this time of year, but now is surely the moment to give it a try. Garnished with pine nuts (which have a similarly provocative reputation), this red, white, and green salad is ideal for Valentine's Day.

For centuries chocolate has been used as an aphrodisiac, linked with all affairs of the heart. For the true romantic desiring a sweet encounter, this seductive Chocolate-Cranberry Torte could be all that's needed to encourage an exchange of promises.

This recipe is an adaptation of a delicious dessert from Jimella Lucas and Nanci Main, co-owners of the Ark Restaurant in Nahcotta, Washington, where cranberries are plentiful.

ABOVE: Crisp on the outside, tender and rosy within, the loin lamb chops are served on a bed of red peppers and mint with rose-shaped potatoes. A hint of love.

CHOCOLATE-CRANBERRY TORTE

SERVES 6 TO 8

³/₄ cup unsweetened cocoa powder, preferably Dutch process
6 tablespoons unsalted butter
1 cup espresso or strong coffee
1¹/₂ cups fresh or frozen cranberries, coarsely chopped
2 cups all-purpose flour
1¹/₂ teaspoons baking soda
¹/₂ teaspoon salt

2 cups sugar
¹/₂ cup buttermilk
2 large eggs, beaten
1 teaspoon vanilla extract
1 cup whipping cream
2 tablespoons confectioners' sugar
¹/₄ cup plus 1 tablespoon framboise

Chocolate Buttercream (page 208)

Chocolate-cranberry torte—
the ultimate aphrodisiac

Preheat the oven to 375° F. Grease and flour two 9-inch cake pans.

Melt the cocoa and butter in the espresso. Toss the cranberries with ½ cup of the flour and set aside. Sift together the remaining flour, baking soda, salt, and sugar. Pour the liquid chocolate mixture into a bowl and gradually add the sifted dry ingredients alternating with the buttermilk. Beat in the eggs and vanilla until smooth. Fold in the cranberries and divide the batter evenly between the two pans. Bake for 25 to 30 minutes or until a cake tester inserted near the center of the layers comes out clean. Cool the cakes for 10 minutes in the pans and then turn out onto wire racks and cool to room temperature. Wrap the cakes well and freeze.

To assemble the cake, unwrap and thaw the cakes for 10 minutes. Combine the whipping cream and confectioners' sugar in a bowl and beat until stiff. Add the tablespoon of framboise and fold it in well.

Using a long serrated knife split each cake into 2 layers. Sprinkle the top of each layer with a little of the ¼ cup of framboise. Place several strips of wax paper around the edges of your cake plate. Center one layer of the cake over the paper strips so that the cake touches the paper all around. Spread one fourth of the buttercream over the first layer and top with another layer. Spread the second layer with some of the flavored whipped cream. Top with the third layer; spread with one third of the remaining buttercream. Finish with the final layer. Spread the remaining buttercream over the sides and top of the torte, forming swirls and peaks with the knife. Remove the wax paper strips. Using a pastry bag fitted with the star-shaped point, decorate the top and around the base of the torte with the remaining flavored whipped cream.

NOTE: For additional garnish, you can decorate with candied violets, cranberries rolled in granulated sugar, or whole mint leaves.

CHOCOLATE BUTTERCREAM

MAKES 4 CUPS

12 ounces semi-sweet
   chocolate, broken into bits
1 tablespoon instant espresso
   (powder)
¼ cup boiling water

6 large egg yolks
3 cups sifted confectioners'
   sugar
2 cups (4 sticks) unsalted
   butter, softened

Melt the chocolate in the top of a partially covered double boiler over barely simmering water. Dissolve the espresso in the boiling water and set aside. Beat the egg yolks with the confectioners' sugar until thick, about 5 minutes. Gradually add the chocolate and then the espresso and beat until smooth. Beating all the time, add the softened butter a little at a time, beating after each addition until smooth. Then beat for 1 to 2 minutes more.

"There is no sight on earth more appealing than the sight of a woman making dinner for someone she loves."
THOMAS WOLFE

Plain
and
Fancy

*L*et's face it, cabbage has a bad reputation, and if you say that you are placing it at the center of dinner for company, someone is going to say or infer with a barely veiled expression of dismay, *"Really?"* Don't be deterred. The cabbage is intrinsically first rate, and stuffed, it is even better. Plumped with mushrooms and walnuts, it truly comes into its own.

This is a high-carbohydrate menu—homey, satisfying, vegetarian, with a good deal of country charm. Cabbage is the "plain" part. Really, it's not so plain as it is comforting. Have you ever noticed, by the way, that friends most often request those half-forgotten recipes that are made simply for comfort?

The fancy part is spice cake, tall and regal, wreathed with walnuts, served beside fresh banana ice cream. Both the cake and the ice cream can stand on their own, but when combined, they are sublime.

M·e·n·u

CABBAGE
STUFFED WITH MUSHROOMS,
WALNUTS, AND BULGUR
·
CARROTS WITH BROWN SUGAR
AND GINGER
·
IRISH SODA BREAD
·
FRESH BANANA ICE CREAM
·
ISLAND SPICE CAKE

ORDER OF PREPARATION

*T*here are quite a few do-ahead steps to this dinner, but not much work once the guests arrive. Begin preparing the meal by making the cake and, while it is baking, make the ice cream. Make the icing and set it aside at room temperature. Wrap the cake well when it is completely cooled and refrigerate it. Ice the cake an hour or so before your guests arrive. The fancy part is now out of the way.

Start blanching the cabbage several hours before dinner. Make the stuffing and sauce. Assemble in a casserole and hold it at room temperature until you are ready to cook it. Start it cooking 30 minutes before you wish to eat.

Make the soda bread 30 minutes before the guests arrive and begin cooking the carrots. Drain the carrots and finish them just before you are ready to sit down. Set everything but dessert on the table at once.

Wine suggestions: Drink a true Alsatian Gewürztraminer or for contrast a spicy Pinot Noir.

❉

CABBAGE STUFFED WITH MUSHROOMS, WALNUTS, AND BULGUR

SERVES 6

1 large head cabbage, regular or Savoy, (about 3 pounds), tough outer leaves removed

3 tablespoons unsalted butter

1 garlic clove, peeled and minced

1 bunch scallions, finely chopped

2 celery stalks, finely chopped

1 pound fresh shiitake mushrooms or white button mushrooms, coarsely chopped

2 cups bulgur, cooked according to package directions

1/4 cup finely chopped fresh parsley

2 tablespoons chopped fresh dill

Salt and freshly ground black pepper to taste

1/4 cup walnuts, toasted for 10 minutes at 350°F. and then coarsely chopped

Tomato-Caraway Coulis (recipe follows)

GARNISH

1/2 cup sour cream

Dill or fennel sprigs

Cut out the deep core of the cabbage and discard it. Bring a large kettle of salted water to a simmer. Add the cabbage and cook until you can easily remove the largest leaves, about 5 minutes. Remove from the kettle and drain well. Carefully separate 12 of the largest leaves and, if not soft enough to roll easily, return them to the pot and cook until tender. Cut out the tough central rib of each leaf. Pat dry and set aside.

Melt the butter in a medium-size skillet, add the garlic, scallions, and celery and sauté until just tender. Add the mushrooms and sauté over medium heat, stirring frequently, until all the liquid has evaporated from the mushrooms. Add the cooked bulgur, parsley, dill, and salt and pepper. Stir in the toasted walnuts and heat thoroughly.

Place the cabbage leaves, curly side up, on a clean flat surface. Fill with 3 to 4 tablespoons of the stuffing. Fold up the bottom edge, fold in both sides, and roll up toward the top edge. Place, seam-side down, in one layer in a large casserole. Add the Tomato-Caraway Coulis, cover, and simmer gently for 30 minutes.

Serve the stuffed cabbage, whole or sliced, accompanied with some of the sauce, sour cream, and a sprig of dill or fennel for garnish.

" 'The time has come,' the Walrus said, 'To talk of many things: of shoes—and ships—and sealing wax— of Cabbages—and Kings . . .' "

LEWIS CARROLL

CHOOSING A CABBAGE: The common green cabbage is fine for all stuffed cabbage recipes but, if you can find it, the ruffled, decorative Savoy makes for a prettier effect. There is no difference in taste or tenderness —just in appearance. But when you are dealing with cabbage, about which some people have a snobbish reluctance, appearance counts for a lot.

"Plain" cabbage stuffed with mushrooms, walnuts, and bulgur—comfort food viewed with a fresh eye

TOMATO-CARAWAY COULIS

MAKES 6 CUPS

½ small onion, finely
   chopped
2 garlic cloves, peeled and
   minced
2 tablespoons unsalted
   butter
1 tablespoon olive oil
4 cups coarsely chopped,
   canned, drained Italian
   plum tomatoes

¼ teaspoon sugar
1 bay leaf
2 teaspoons caraway seeds
1 1-inch piece dried orange
   peel (available in your
   spice section)
1 tablespoon tomato paste
   Salt and freshly ground
   black pepper to taste

In a saucepan, sauté the onion and garlic in the butter and olive oil until tender but not brown. Stir in the tomatoes, sugar, bay leaf, caraway seeds, and orange peel. Cook, covered, over low heat for 10 minutes; then uncover, add the tomato paste, and cook for 10 to 15 minutes more. Discard the bay leaf and orange peel. Use as is, or force through a food mill fitted with a medium blade. Correct the seasoning with salt and pepper.

CARROTS WITH BROWN SUGAR AND GINGER

SERVES 6

1½ pounds whole baby
   carrots, peeled
3 tablespoons unsalted
   butter

2 tablespoons dark brown
   sugar
½ teaspoon ground ginger

Put the carrots in a saucepan with ½ cup of water. Cook the carrots until just tender, 8 to 10 minutes. Drain and set aside.

Melt the butter with the brown sugar and ginger in the same saucepan. Return the carrots to the pan and toss with the sugar mixture for 2 to 3 minutes or until caramelized. Serve immediately.

"The trick to living happily is learning to enjoy the small pleasures. You can't wait for the big ones because they don't come along often enough. Fixing dinner is a readily available small pleasure. You can be creative, you can please someone else, you can enjoy the food."
STANTON DELAPLANE

IRISH SODA BREAD

MAKES 2 LOAVES

4 cups all-purpose flour
4 tablespoons unsalted
  butter
1 teaspoon baking soda
1 tablespoon baking
  powder

2 tablespoons sugar
½ teaspoon salt
2 tablespoons caraway
  seeds
1 large egg
1¾ cups buttermilk

Preheat the oven to 375° F.

In a large mixing bowl, combine the flour and butter, working it with your fingers until it has the consistency of coarse meal. Blend in the baking soda, baking powder, sugar, salt, and caraway seeds. Beat the egg and buttermilk together in another bowl. Make a well in the center of the dry ingredients and add the liquid ingredients. Stir just to blend.

Lightly dust a clean surface with flour and knead the dough for 3 to 4 minutes or until smooth. Form the dough into two round loaves and, using a sharp knife, cut a ¼-inch-deep cross on the top of each loaf. Bake on greased baking sheets, placed 3 inches apart, for 30 to 35 minutes. Cool on wire racks for 10 to 15 minutes before slicing.

❄

FRESH BANANA ICE CREAM

SERVES 6

1 cup sugar
1 tablespoon cornstarch
2 cups milk
3 large eggs, beaten
1 cup heavy cream

1 teaspoon dark rum
3 medium-size very ripe
  bananas, mashed with 1
  tablespoon lemon juice

Combine the sugar, cornstarch, and milk in a medium-size saucepan over low heat. Cook for 2 minutes or until the mixture thickens slightly. Stir a little of the hot milk into the beaten eggs; then add the eggs to the milk mixture. Cook for 2 to 3 minutes more, stirring all the time, until smooth and thick. Stir in the cream, rum, and bananas and lemon juice. Cool. Pour into an ice-cream maker and freeze according to the manufacturer's instructions.

A quick bread, made without yeast.

"Plain cooking cannot be entrusted to plain cooks."
COUNTESS MORPHY

*Island spice cake with caramel frosting
served with banana ice cream—an
elegant and delicious combination*

ISLAND SPICE CAKE

SERVES 6

2½ cups sifted cake flour
2 teaspoons baking powder
½ teaspoon baking soda
¼ teaspoon salt
2 teaspoons ground
   cinnamon
¼ teaspoon ground nutmeg
¼ teaspoon ground allspice
¼ teaspoon ground mace
1 teaspoon ground cloves

½ cup (1 stick) unsalted
   butter, softened
¼ cup vegetable shortening
1 cup packed dark brown
   sugar
3 large eggs, beaten
1 cup buttermilk
   Caramel Frosting (recipe
   follows)
6 to 8 walnuts

Preheat the oven to 350° F. Grease two 8-inch-round cake pans.

Sift together the flour, baking powder, baking soda, salt, and spices; then sift again.

In a separate bowl, cream together the butter, shortening, and sugar until light and fluffy. Add the eggs and beat thoroughly. Add the dry ingredients to this mixture alternating with the buttermilk, blending after each addition only enough to thoroughly mix. Pour into prepared pans and bake for 35 to 40 minutes. Let cool for 10 minutes in the pans before turning out on wire racks to cool completely.

Frost the cake with the Caramel Frosting and decorate the top with the walnuts.

CARAMEL FROSTING

MAKES 3 CUPS

½ cup (1 stick) unsalted
   butter
⅓ cup packed dark brown
   sugar

2 tablespoons molasses
2 cups confectioners' sugar
¼ cup heavy cream

Heat the butter, brown sugar, and molasses together over low heat in a medium-size saucepan until the butter is liquid and the sugar has dissolved. Cool. Beat in the confectioners' sugar and the heavy cream alternately, a little at a time, until the frosting is just smooth and thick enough to spread.

Cry Fowl

*I*f you are looking for a way out of winter, if you are longing for spring, here is a dinner with hints of all that you are waiting for. Fresh mustard greens, first harbingers of the vernal season, are here, and garden peas if you can find them, and an eclectic blend of dishes that are light and brightly colored, with a whiff of the exotic. Serve each course separately to savor all the spice and flavor. The familiars of the menu are laced with the unexpected, and everything together is attractive, original, enticing. Dessert is substantial, not industrial-weight, but substantial enough to fend off the lingering cold.

Some of the food makes a few demands on the cook in the hour before the dinner. Nothing is difficult, but there is a lot of last-minute assembly and finishing, and the menu works well in a large, open kitchen where friends can talk and watch you cook and maybe lend a helping hand frying the chicken or keeping an eye on the pasta.

ORDER OF PREPARATION

*Y*ou can make the saffron sauce, the cumin cream, and the apple compote before everyone arrives and then reheat them. Made on the morning of the dinner, the gingerbread takes only a few minutes and is best eaten the day it's made. Wash the salad greens and make the dressing while the gingerbread bakes and keep the greens refrigerated. Have all the necessary equipment for the rest of the meal ready in advance and chop and measure your ingredients before you begin.

Start by boiling the water for the orzo. Soak the chicken breast strips. Finish the orzo. (Incidentally, the egg-pasta orzo is so savory it can stand on its own as a first course, or serve as an accompaniment.) Start heating the oil for the chicken as you sit down to eat or make the chicken ahead and keep it warm in the oven. Serve the chicken and then the salad. If you like, warm the gingerbread and apple compote before serving them.

Wine suggestion: Try a fine, fruity Chardonnay.

CHICKEN BREASTS WITH CUMIN CREAM

SERVES 6

3 whole chicken breasts, split, deboned, and skinned, or buy 6 chicken cutlets
1 cup milk
2 cups all-purpose flour
Salt and freshly ground black pepper to taste
1 teaspoon ground cumin
2 to 3 cups peanut oil

SAUCE
3 cups heavy cream

1½ tablespoons Dijon mustard
1 tablespoon ground cumin
2 garlic cloves, smashed and peeled
¼ cup chicken stock
Salt and freshly ground black pepper to taste
3 tablespoons unsalted butter

GARNISH
Fresh chive strips

Pound the chicken breasts slightly and cut them into thin strips. Soak the strips for 10 minutes in the milk. Drain. Combine the flour, salt, pepper, and cumin. Toss the chicken in the seasoned flour to coat lightly. Place the chicken strips in a colander and agitate to remove any excess flour.

Heat the oil in a deep frying pan or wok until hot but not smoking. Fry the chicken pieces for 3 to 4 minutes or until golden. Transfer to a warm platter lined with paper towels and keep warm in a low oven until ready to serve. If you wish, the strips may be refried for a scant minute just before serving.

Prepare the sauce. In a medium-size saucepan, reduce the heavy cream by one third over high heat. Whisk in the mustard, cumin, garlic, and chicken stock. Season with salt and pepper. Do not oversalt if you are using canned stock. Simmer the sauce for 5 minutes; then turn the heat to low and swirl in the butter, 1 tablespoon at a time, until well blended. Divide the sauce between 6 warm plates and top with mounds of crisp chicken pieces. Decorate with strips of fresh chives.

"... The French when in doubt always answer chicken."
ALICE B. TOKLAS

*Crisp golden chicken breasts
served with cumin cream—
a winning combination*

ORZO WITH PEAS AND SAFFRON-BASIL SAUCE

SERVES 6

¼ teaspoon finely chopped shallots

⅓ cup dry white wine

¼ cup white wine vinegar

¼ teaspoon crumbled saffron threads

⅓ cup heavy cream

1½ cups (3 sticks) unsalted butter

Salt to taste

¾ cup finely shredded fresh basil

1 pound orzo

2 cups fresh peas or 1 10-ounce package frozen peas

1 bunch scallions, finely cut on the diagonal

To make the saffron sauce, in a small saucepan, combine the shallots, wine, and vinegar. Bring to a simmer and add the saffron. Reduce by two thirds over medium-high heat. Stir in the heavy cream and again reduce by two thirds. Turn the heat to low and add the butter, 1 tablespoon at a time, whisking after each addition. Do not let the sauce get hot enough for the butter to separate and liquefy. Remove from the heat, season with salt, and add the shredded basil. Set aside.

Bring a large kettle of salted water to a boil. Add the orzo and cook according to the package directions. Drain well and transfer to a large skillet. If you are using frozen peas, rinse them under cold running water to thaw them. Drain well. Add the peas and the scallions to the orzo. Add the saffron sauce and heat over low heat, tossing frequently, until hot.

Greens and tangerines—the perfect winter salad

GREENS AND TANGERINES

SERVES 6

DRESSING

1 garlic clove, peeled and minced

1 medium-size shallot, minced

¼ cup balsamic vinegar

¼ cup freshly squeezed orange juice

Salt and freshly ground black pepper to taste

1 tablespoon finely chopped fresh parsley

¼ cup olive oil

6 cups assorted lettuces, such as red leaf, Bibb, curly endive, escarole, and dandelion, washed and torn into bite-size pieces

½ red onion, thinly sliced

1 cup wild mustard (leaves and flowers) or arugula

6 tangerines, peeled, seeded, and sectioned

Combine all the ingredients for the dressing, except the oil, in a bowl. Add the oil, whisking all the time until blended and emulsified. In another bowl, toss the greens and red onion with two thirds of the dressing and arrange on individual plates. Place the mustard leaves and tangerines around the edge. Scatter a few mustard flowers over each plate and drizzle with the remaining dressing.

Apple compote and gingerbread— old-fashioned freshness

GINGERBREAD WITH A DUSTING OF SNOW

SERVES 6

1 cup molasses
½ cup water
5 tablespoons unsalted
  butter
½ cup packed dark brown
  sugar
2 cups cake flour
1 tablespoon ground ginger

½ teaspoon ground
  cinnamon
½ teaspoon ground cloves
½ teaspoon salt
1 teaspoon baking soda
  Confectioners' sugar for
  dusting

Preheat the oven to 350° F. Grease a 9 × 9 × 2-inch baking pan.

In a small saucepan, combine the molasses, water, butter, and brown sugar and heat slowly, stirring occasionally, until the butter has melted. Stir until well mixed and smooth. Set aside to cool.

In a mixing bowl, combine all the remaining ingredients, except the confectioners' sugar. When the molasses mixture has cooled, stir it into the dry ingredients and beat well. Turn into the prepared pan and bake for 20 to 25 minutes or until the top springs back when pressed lightly with a fingertip. Serve warm, dusted with the sugar.

APPLE COMPOTE

SERVES 6

4 large baking apples, such
  as McIntosh or Jonathan,
  peeled, cored, and cubed
2 tablespoons sugar

½ cup water
  Grated rind of 1 navel
  orange or 1 lemon

Combine all the ingredients in a large noncorrodible saucepan and cook, uncovered, until just tender. Do not cook down as far as you would for applesauce. Mash the apples slightly and serve warm or chilled.

"It's
**bad luck to peel peaches, pears,
or apples alone."**

Index